AEROSMITH

WHAT IT TAKES

AEROSMITH

WHAT IT TAKES

Dave Bowler

B🍃XTREE

First published 1997 by Boxtree Limited,
an imprint of Macmillan Publishers Ltd
25 Eccleston Place, London SW1W 9NF
and Basingstoke.

Associated companies throughout the world

ISBN 0 7522 2243 0

Cover design: Shoot That Tiger!

Front cover photos: Redferns

Picture Credits

Kirkland/Retna: page 5 *top*
Taylor/Retna: page 5 *bottom*
Davila/Retna: page 6 *bottom*
Mottram/Retna: page 7 *bottom*
Van Iperen/Retna: page 8

9 8 7 6 5 4 3 2 1

Typeset by SX Composing DTP, Rayleigh, Essex
Printed and bound by Mackays of Chatham plc, Kent

A CIP catalogue record for this book is available from the British Library.

CONTENTS

Introduction   1

Chapter One: One Way   4

Chapter Two: Hey Hey, We're the Hookers   15

Chapter Three: Makin' It   23

Chapter Four: Round and Round . . . and Round   30

Chapter Five: Nobody's Fault?   39

Chapter Six: Dumb and Dumber   52

Chapter Seven: Dead in the Water   62

Chapter Eight: When Push Comes to Shove   73

Chapter Nine: Roll Up, Roll Up for the
                Resurrection Shuffle   84

Chapter Ten: Here Comes the Cavalry   91

Chapter Eleven: Pump-Action 45s   105

Chapter Twelve: Eat the Who?   117

Chapter Thirteen: Can't Stop Messin'   126

Discography   130

Sources   134

DEDICATION

To Mom and Dad
For taking care of everything.
And for Denise
Not for just an hour, not for just a day . . .
Always

David

To Trish, Emma and Rebecca
For all their love and support.
And Mum, Dad, Joyce and Wal
For all their help and patience.

Bryan

ACKNOWLEDGEMENTS

In traditional fashion, we'd like to extend our thanks to a variety of people who have given succour during the researching and writing of the tome now before you. As usual, Tanja Howarth and Mark Hayward have put up with a great deal of aimless whinging without losing their sense of humour, and the same is true of everyone at Boxtree.

Thanks to go to *Hot Press, Q, Vox, Sounds* and *Rolling Stone*, whose many and varied articles on the long and tortured history of Aerosmith were a great help.

Finally, if you want to find any fellow Aerosmith fans, send an SAE to Kate at Midlands Metal International, 47 Thackeray Walk, Stafford, Staffordshire, ST17 9SE.

INTRODUCTION

'Our story is that we had it all and we pissed it away.' Guitarist Joe Perry's summation of the first decade of Aerosmith's career is precise and to the point. By 1977, Aerosmith were a band that could fill the biggest stadiums all over the USA with the greatest of ease, a band that played shows to crowds of 350,000, a band that could release an album in the knowledge that it would go gold, probably platinum as a million-seller, and become ensconced in the *Billboard* top ten. In the US, it would have been difficult to think of any bigger or any better rock 'n' roll band, all the competition coming from this side of the water in the form of The Rolling Stones or Led Zeppelin. Within five short years, Perry had left his toxic twin Steven Tyler to pilot the band alone, and Aerosmith had become a sad joke, synonymous with the bad old days of the 1970s, when bands spiralled out of control beneath a heady but ultimately poisonous cocktail of drink and drugs.

That there is still an Aerosmith story to tell in the late 1990s is remarkable enough for the five members of the group are all lucky still to be around. That they are a band as musically vibrant and exciting as at any time in their career, that they now enjoy worldwide popularity which eclipses anything they achieved on a purely Stateside basis in the halcyon days of *Rocks*, and that they are currently basking in the security of one of the most generous recording contracts of all time is almost unbelievable. Good God, they've even been immortalised on *The Simpsons*!

1

In spite of the important contributions made by Brad Whitford, Tom Hamilton and Joey Kramer, it is the musical fulcrum of Steven Tyler and Joe Perry that has provided the sparks that have fired Aerosmith over almost thirty years. It was also Tyler's and Perry's appetite for destruction which almost killed the band. On and off stage, their combustible relationship has been anything but tranquil, although it's that very tempestuousness that has taken the band through the peaks and troughs that have characterised their career. Like the Glimmer Twins, Mick Jagger and Keith Richards, with whom they were so regularly compared, each has eventually been driven to the conclusion that musically they can't function without the other. Just as the Stones were fortified by a spate of unsuccessful and unfulfilling solo albums in the late 1980s, Aerosmith had earlier regrouped when Perry's defection helped them realise that the band was greater than the sum of its parts and that none could function properly away from its protective umbrella. Aided by new management and a new record company, Tyler and Perry were able to realign their attitudes and, from being a malignant force, Aerosmith became a rock to which they could cling as they put their own lives back in order, their main inspiration being a need to repeat, even surpass former glories.

It seemed their greatest legacy might be the bands they had inspired – Van Halen, Def Leppard, Jane's Addiction and Guns N' Roses (who *Time* magazine called an Aerosmith for the 1990s) – rather than any of their own songs. Yet, fiercely competitive, overbearingly ambitious, the fact that Aerosmith looked set to be relegated to a mere footnote in the history of rock 'n' roll rankled even as they plumbed the depths of drink and drug abuse. Aerosmith, who had been musical giants, poised to replace Led Zeppelin as the premier hard rock band in the world, were now the forgotten men. Reaching rock bottom in 1983, not only were they a collection of physical and mental wrecks all but destroyed by their voracious consumption of the rock 'n' roll lifestyle, they were flat broke too. Steven Tyler, who had been as recognisable a face as any in the US just four years earlier, was now living in squalor in The Gorham Hotel in New York City just so that he would be close to 8th Avenue where 'I could score a couple of $20 bags of junk, hoping the dealers would recognise me so

I might get a bit more.' Indicative of his fractured state of mind at the time, he said, 'Even then, I'd always pick up one of those pitta-pocket health food sandwiches, something that was really good for me.'

To come back from so far down takes a little luck, some good friends and a lot of courage and resolution. Fortunately, Aerosmith have always had what it takes . . .

1

ONE WAY

Was there ever a better decade to be a teenager than the 1960s? This was, after all, the first full decade in which teenagers really made their presence felt, following in the wake of their post-Presley emergence. This was the era where kids all over the Western world had money for the first time, a time when all manner of supposedly benevolent substances began to seep into the cultural consciousness, a time of free love when sexual promiscuity wasn't only tolerated but actively encouraged.

While all that was taking place, there was a soundtrack unravelling in the background, the like of which had never been heard before. The 1960s offered some of the greatest music ever made for, in keeping with the burgeoning excitement and air of experimentation that characterised the times, rock 'n' roll was being invented literally before the eyes of a rapt audience. There were no rules, no boundaries, only limitless possibilities. And, for those teenagers who would become the next generation of rockers, the bands that would capitalise on this explosion a decade later, there was an added bonus. Groups like The Beatles, The Who and The Rolling Stones were telling a disbelieving world that rock 'n' roll could be a lucrative career. When The Beatles started out, no one thought they'd survive more than a couple of years. It wouldn't be long before Ringo would have to retire to the hairdressing salon he talked of opening. By the time *Help!* was released in 1965, it was obvious that rock music was here to stay and that those with a talent for it could turn it into a very good living indeed. And, aside from becoming a politician or working for the CIA, what better way was there of laying your hands on untold quantities of money, drink, drugs and sex? Your mother still mightn't have liked seeing you wasting your time with a guitar, but even she knew that one day that guitar might buy you a big, shiny Cadillac. No generation of teenagers had ever had such an opportunity open up before them. Of course, not all of the kids needed any encouragement . . .

Steven Tallarico was born in New York City on 26 March 1948, the perfect age to have his musical curiosity roused by Elvis and then satisfied by the Stones. Music was always the number-one attraction for a boy who soon made it obvious that he was a born performer. Living a schizophrenic existence through his early years, the week was spent in the Bronx where his father was a music teacher, while weekends and summers were spent in the idyllic environment of Sunapee, New Hampshire, where the Tallaricos owned the very successful Trow-Rico resort hotel.

The family had a musical background, for not only was Steven's father a musician, his grandfather Giovanni had been an accomplished cellist, touring all over the US throughout the 1920s and 1930s. It was Steven's father who had the greatest influence on him, however, filling the family home with music. 'He's the one who turned me on. It was his piano. He used to teach lessons, so he'd have practice going on all day. I was a kid then and I'd sit under the piano. Got it drummed into my head so to speak.' Steven practised his chops at the piano, but it was the rhythm at least as much as the melody that really made an impression on him, maybe a legacy of listening to the piano from beneath, hearing the key hammers beating out their own tune independent of the notes they were creating.

The precocious kid soon wanted to show people what he could do, demanding their attention. As an infant, he staged his own shows at the Trow-Rico before indulgently appreciative family audiences, and as he grew up he soon graduated to playing in other hotels alongside his father in his society swing band. 'I used to play drums with him up in New Hampshire and had to wax my hair back with Pomatex or whatever they call it. You'll never see that picture!' By now, the Tallaricos, worried by the increasing violence that was becoming a feature of life in the Bronx, had moved out to Yonkers where Steven's father now taught music at Roosevelt High, the educational establishment where Steven himself would have to study. Though a fiercely intelligent and inquisitive child, school was nothing but a pain to an independently minded youngster who was already looking for something else. In 1964, at the age of sixteen, that something arrived in the shape of five insolent blues-playing kids from England. 'I saw 'em on TV that year, late at night, one of those talk shows. There were the Stones looking dumb as you please, but great! I said, "Yessss! Someone's doing it!" Pretty soon, we had a whole clique of people from school who loved the Stones. We used to go to a hotel room in the same hotel upstairs from them. That's how crazy we were. My friend was a ringer for Brian Jones and y'know who I pass for. We came driving down the street and the fuckin' kids nearly turned the car over, broke the windshield, ripped the antenna off.'

Steven had already graduated to his first band by now, a group evolving out of the Green Mountain Boys gang that he ran with. 'It was like a club, y'know. Otherwise you just weren't cool!' Tallarico was hammering away on the drums at the back, the band having adopted the moniker of The Strangeurs, before changing that to Chain Reaction. Steven recalled, 'When we first saw the Stones, I wasn't lead singing, I never had any idea I'd be doing that. I was playing drums and all of a sudden, we were doing that Beach Boys thing, "In My Room", in my basement in Yonkers and they were singing so bad I went, "Gimme that!" Brought the mike over, I started singing behind the drums and it worked out quite well for the longest time."

The impact Mick Jagger had on Tallarico can't be underestimated. It wasn't simply that the Stones supposedly represented the longer-haired, badly behaved version of the lovable Fab Four, a fact that appealed to his sense of rebellious chic. What really moved him was the fact that the Stones had a singer that was a dead ringer for his adolescent self. Having had a tough time in school, the kids taunting him over his huge mouth and distinctive features, here was someone who looked the same and who just happened to be about the coolest guy in the universe. Any last inhibitions that he might have had about his looks flew out of the window. The final obstacle between him and rock stardom had been removed. Who wanted to be the anonymous drummer when you could be the singer and capture everybody's attention? Fortune was great, but Steven wanted fame every bit as badly, for, as a child of Italian lineage, he was inevitably set apart from the mainstream way of American WASP life. Like so many immigrants before and since, Steven believed that the only way to fit in to that society was to succeed, to make it so big that everyone would want a piece of him, so everything that Steven did, he had to do to the max. There was no room for half measures in anything. Young Tallarico saw rock 'n' roll as his vehicle, the fame associated with it the passport to a future where he would be accepted into the bosom of the US.

Even though he wanted to be the focal point of the band, his instinctive feel for rhythm meant that he had to continue as the drummer, working out his own method of singing while he was playing. Belting out lyrics over the sound of the drums was tough, but it provided him with an excellent grounding in performing live as a singer, strengthening his vocal chords, helping him become ever more powerful – it was a similar apprenticeship to that which Robert Plant was enduring at the same time in the Band of Joy, though in his case he was having to sing over the cacophonous volume created by John Bonham in tiny clubs with extremely limited PA equipment. As Chain Reaction played more and more shows, so Steven honed his voice to the point at which he had absolute control over the full range of its possibilities, in both volume and tonal colour. Tallarico was very rapidly becoming a musical force to be reckoned with.

His greatest problem was that he couldn't make it alone, and although Chain Reaction opened shows for bands like The Rascals and the Lovin' Spoonful and even got so far as cutting their own record, it was apparent that they were never going to take the US by storm. Consequently, Steven fell in and out with other groups, Chain Reaction ending in violence in Southampton: Tallarico, tired of playing in the swanky resort, leapt over his drum kit and tried to strangle the guitarist! He continued as a singing drummer in an outfit called William Proud which regularly played in New Hampshire throughout the tail end of the decade but without making any real impact. Achieving the holy grail of musical acceptance was becoming increasingly important after his schooling had come to a premature end.

Any kid dabbling in bands in the 1960s was likely to be exposed to drugs sooner or later. A bundle of nervous energy with a compulsive, addictive nature, Steven was desperate to try anything that was available. So perhaps it was always inevitable that he would get thrown out of Roosevelt High for being caught in possession of grass, a source of great embarrassment to his father. Steven felt equally resentful and protested that he was set up, arguing, 'An undercover nark infiltrated my ceramics class, believe it or not. The scumbag sold lids of grass to me, and some other kids then busted us for possession.' He did admit to a partiality for illicit substances though, saying, 'I started taking drugs when I was sixteen because it was the natural thing for anyone growing up in my home town to do.' One repercussion was that he was then 'classified as a 1Y, a youthful offender by the draft board. Gimme a break! At least it meant I didn't have to go to Vietnam.' He ended up in an establishment called Quintano's, which specialised in 'the creative child who couldn't get on with the system'. In some ways it sounded ideal, for Steven was undoubtedly creative and he couldn't fit in with the regimentation of the traditional school curriculum which held little of interest for him. He wanted to be making music, not learning algebra, so Quintano's seemed to hold promise. In reality though, it comprised all the misfits who had disrupted classes in their previous schools. Tallarico's period there was wasted.

He still found plenty of time to get into trouble, including his first really serious brush with the law. 'Someone told me it wasn't Brian Jones playing recorder on "Ruby Tuesday" so I pushed him out the window. Spent the weekend in jail and wrote my first blues song – ah, sweet revenge!'

In 1969, Woodstock formed the focal point of the rock year and, as you'd expect, Tallarico made it there too. 'I went with a friend. Someone stole the gas cap to the car, it rained and the tank got full of water and we couldn't leave! It looked like a war zone when they'd all gone. I still have a cola cooler that I'd stolen and there's a banner that hung behind us at Woodstock with a stick figure holding a cornucopia with a dick or a tail between his legs. I stole that there, too. After everyone had gone, I stole all the banners that were left and had them duplicated – that's what we used later on in 1971 for our backdrops when we did all those clubs in New York.'

With school now consigned to the bin, Steven drifted aimlessly for a while. He helped out at Trow-Rico – 'I worked the land. I used to mow the lawn, build roads, dig out ponds. That's why I have the frame I have. It's from getting up early and busting my hump.' While he was in New York, he briefly roadied for the Beck and Page incarnation of The Yardbirds. It was this brief association that inadvertently led to what became one of Steven's trademarks – his use of long, flowing scarves draped around the microphone stand. 'I was living with a woman on 23rd Street in New York. Chain Reaction was playing The Scene, opening for Tiny Tim, and I had no shirt. This woman left me for Jimmy Page when I was working for The Yardbirds when they came through, and she took all my clothes and threw them out. I found them in an alley. I took one of the shirts and tied it to the mike stand. It was all ripped. I kind of liked that, those flowy things that I copped from Brian Jones, so I started wrapping scarves round there.' This was further evidence that the look and imagery employed in British rock 'n' roll captivated Tallarico every bit as much as its sound. He recalled, 'When I was a kid, we used to get these British imports like The Pretty Things and to see those picture sleeves, the way they dressed and were covered with all that hair, man, I was knocked out by that.'

Mainly though, Steven spent his time at Sunapee, playing up to the part of the rock 'n' roller about to make it big. He remembered later, 'In my mind I was always a rock star, I would pretend I knew what it was like to be in an established band. I still have clippings from my first group when we were The Strangeurs – "Steven Tallarico, his lower lip hanging like Jagger's brought the front row to its feet." I was sixteen, playing rock star even when the music sounded like bad Freddie And The Dreamers.'

Away from the rock scene, one of the regular haunts where Steven liked to hang out was an ice-cream parlour called The Anchorage. One member of staff there remembered him and his behaviour very clearly. 'Steven came up to Sunapee with these bands like Chain Reaction, wearing clothes from Carnaby Street and this real long hair.

They were loud and obnoxious, behaving like rock stars are supposed to behave, especially when they're in a little town and nobody knows how not-so-big they are. They'd come into The Anchorage and throw food and shit, and I'd have to clean up after them.'

If Steven thought he was impressing this small-town employee with his loutishness, he was sadly mistaken because Joe Perry knew plenty about the music business and he knew damn well that the bands Steven had been in were hopeless. 'His music lacked guts. When they played stuff from The Beatles' *White Album*, it just made you think how good The Beatles were.'

Perry was two and a half years younger than Steven, born in Massachusetts on 10 September 1950. Like the loud-mouthed singer, Joe had had his troubles at school, never settling in, having few friends and keeping himself to himself. A brooding personality, he just wanted to stay at home, locked in his room, strumming the cheap Sears Silverstone guitar his parents had bought for him. Worried about his lack of academic progress, they moved him into a high-class prep school but nothing could inspire him except for the latest batch of rock records. To demonstrate his utter distaste for the education system, he quit school a week before graduation, taking a dead-end job in a foundry for $2 an hour so that he could scrape together enough cash to buy himself a real guitar. When his parents moved out to New Hampshire, Joe went with them, tearing himself away from his own band, Flash, which had started in the final days at high school. He earned his keep at The Anchorage and topped up his meagre wage by playing guitar in a new group, initially known as Pipe Dream, later taking the name The Jam Band. By the late 1960s, Perry had become a real authority on rock music and had his own very clear ideas on just what kind of music he wanted to play.

After the initial British invasion which had centred around Merseybeat, the music took on a much harder edge with The Beatles, The Who and the Stones still in the vanguard, and with the lighter, poppier acts such as Gerry and the Pacemakers, The Dave Clark Five and Herman's Hermits falling by the wayside. They were replaced by artists steeped in American blues mythology; raucous, powerhouse bands such as Cream, Alvin Lee's Ten Years After and The Yardbirds.

Given that the blues was a peculiarly American kind of music, created on the Mississippi delta by the descendants of the slaves, it was remarkable that in the 1960s almost all of the great blues bands were made up of white Englishmen – often highly privileged ones at that. A music that was so indigenously part of the black American experience seemed like it should be the sole preserve of those who had lived that life, yet there seemed to be very few such musicians around, with only a very select band such as B.B. King and John Lee Hooker making a name for themselves on the wider scene. The truth was that blues was an exciting, emotionally effecting music so it was little surprise that people of every colour and creed could get something from it. But black artists found it incredibly difficult to push past the prejudices of the day and take their place on centre stage. Motown was accepted because it was pure, harmless pop, but the idea of a black man singing the blues, articulating the catalogue of wrongs that had been perpetrated on him and his people, was viewed by some as being very dangerous in the way that rap music was in the 1980s. A bunch of white guys from Kent or Liverpool weren't to be feared, their music was something to be celebrated.

At the same time, white English musicians weren't tethered by the reverence that American musicians had for the blues. Youngsters like Tallarico and Perry had greater access to the real McCoy, the genuine roots of the British beat sound; if the black man's blues weren't commercially pushed, it did exist and you could get hold of it. Maybe English musicians such as John Myall, Jimmy Page, Eric Clapton, Peter Green, Paul McCartney, Keith Richards and Jeff Beck felt freer to experiment with the blues, were less worried about bastardising it, crossing it with pop, jazz or even with British music hall traditions, to create their own hybrid. Americans, especially white Americans, would approach such an operation with real trepidation, fearful of the backlash that might accompany it. Authenticity was all.

What that meant in practical terms was that English artists had a stranglehold on the rock world. They were the kings, but their inevitable absences from US concert stages made it very obvious that if only an American band could come along and play in the same spirit with their own attitude, they would clean up. It was only a matter of time before someone did it, as Joe Perry realised. 'We were hearing English bands like Peter Green's Fleetwood Mac. Once we got going, we were like the Stones on an obvious superficial level, but musically I always saw us as a lot more like The Yardbirds. There weren't many white Stateside combos performing it big through Marshalls and all that, and we wanted to be the first American equivalent.' Consequently, when Perry's The Jam Band got on stage, they played it hard.

One of his colleagues was bassist Tom Hamilton, who'd been born in Colorado on 31 December 1951. Hamilton had travelled the country with his parents – his father, an Air Force worker, being regularly transferred from base to base. They had pitched up in New Hampshire in the mid 1960s. Like Tallarico and Perry, Tom had trouble with school and was busted for possession of acid. Again, like the others' misdemeanours, if didn't bother him much, treating it as all part of the rock 'n' roll experience in which he was thoroughly immersed.

Hamilton was an inveterate gig-goer throughout the 1960s and he even remembered seeing Chain Reaction play in New York in 1965. He didn't think much of the band; they weren't great, but the singer 'was such a fuckin' pro – he was the real thing'. With that memory still fresh, Hamilton was delighted to find that Tallarico was a regular in The Anchorage, and he and Perry set about inviting him along to see one of The Jam Band's gigs at The Barn in Sunapee. Tallarico, who by now considered himself to be the consummate professional, was amazed by what he saw. 'Joe couldn't sing at all but when I heard that booah dang booah dum, ah man, my dick went sooo hard! You can't learn to get good like that, you play what you got. I heard The Jam Band, they had a lot of raunch and I figured I could take a step back and gradually build with them. They got up and did "Rattle-snake Shake" and I said to myself, "That's it. These guys suck but they have got it going, and that's better than any fuck I ever had." I knew if I could show them a little of what I knew, with the looseness they had, we'd have something.'

Perry and Hamilton were well aware of their potential, the two of them locking together to produce a solid groove, but they knew that they lacked any kind of instrumental discipline that would be essential in enabling them to take their music to any wider audience.

Perry confessed, 'The Jam Band didn't give a shit about melody. Just enough to give us an excuse to play. I liked to create mayhem and go crazy and that was what Steven liked about me and the band when he first saw me. Steven was into arrangements and getting things right. They had to be perfect, he had to have a feeling of control. That was the combination that made Aerosmith Aerosmith. I was the unholy terror and he was the restraint. That caused constant fights. I wouldn't mind going on to the stage without having anything ready because then you might get something really, really good out of it. Steven would get pissed if I didn't take the same lead every time. Boring!'

Joe's early assessment of Steven as someone who liked everything to be in its place was uncannily accurate. Fascinated by the tight, intricate arrangements of The Beatles, he had an intuitive understanding of musical theory, understandable given his father's background. Although rock 'n' roll might seem and sound chaotic, it could, like all music, be virtually reduced to the level of mathematical formulae, strands of sound intertwining in very specific patterns. However, such a crass reduction of the rhythms and melodies failed to do justice to the indefinable magic that distinguished the great from the humdrum. If understanding the effect that the simple repetition of notes or the positioning of chord changes could have was important in the songwriting process, more crucial still was an attitude that allowed the triggering of emotional reactions. One of the most memorable pieces of musical criticism which betrayed this fundamental misunderstanding of rock's primitive attractions came in *The Times* in December 1963 when William Mann discussed the use of pandiatonic clusters, Aeolian cadences, mediant and submediant switches evident in Lennon and McCartney's songwriting. Their (unconscious) use of such devices suggested that they had turned songwriting into a science, but the rough desperation of Lennon's voice and the utterly unselfconscious exuberance evident in McCartney's playing made it obvious that they still felt it was an emotional art.

Steven Tallarico had already mastered the science of songwriting, convinced that in his compulsive perfectionism lay the seeds of his future success. In a sense he was right, for his attention to detail and his analytical approach to both writing and performance proved crucial in the long run, but so rigidly did he hold on to those beliefs he couldn't yet relax his grip sufficiently to embrace the art of rock 'n' roll – its spontaneity, the dishevelled, if cultivated, sloppiness that defined that nebulous, yet vital commodity, 'cool', the very thing that would mark him out from the competition. It would be up to Joe Perry and Tom Hamilton to help him complete his education.

2

HEY HEY, WE'RE THE HOOKERS

Fortunately for the sake of each fragile performer's ego, neither Perry nor Tallarico was the finished article when they met. Both still had much they could learn from one another. Given his comparatively elevated status in the rock milieu, it is to his credit that Tallarico realised this and could admit to it. Above all, it was very apparent he had to lighten up, relinquish the precious hold he kept on the music and let it flow from him. Seeing that Perry and Hamilton could offer him a lot in that direction, he set about investigating The Jam Band further.

At the time he first saw them, Tallarico was busy trying to further his own career as both a singer and songwriter. Perry remembered, 'Tom and I were just jamming down at The Barn and Steven was there on his own and said he had to do a demo tape for an audition. He asked us to back him on The Beatles' "I'm Down" and that was the first time Tom and I had been on tape. It was a lot of fun and it was the start of things. That's why when years later we were looking for a cover to do on *Permanent Vacation*, that seemed like a good thing to do.'

Tallarico slotted in alongside the Perry/Hamilton axis and it was immediately obvious to them all that this line up had immense potential. Tom Hamilton remembered that they were so excited about having played on Steven's tape, they rushed off to repeat the experience. 'We wanted to hear ourselves on a record so we worked up a few Jeff Beck songs, recorded 'em on a two-track tape recorder

15

and took 'em out to Ace Recording Studios in Boston and had 'em make up some acetates for us. I didn't know then that you could only play 'em ten times or something before they wore out!'

Tallarico replaced The Jam Band drummer Pudge Scott, but that was just a temporary move, as he had no intention of being stuck at the back forever. Rock star Tallarico wanted to get out front as quick as possible. The next recruit to the band was a rhythm guitarist, Ray Tabano, who had known Steven for the best part of a decade, joining forces with him in William Proud. Given that it was Steven who was joining the Perry/Hamilton group, it's testament to his forceful personality that he was able to shift the whole emphasis from a Cream-like power trio to what was the classical – Stones influenced – rock set-up featuring twin guitarists. It was pretty obvious that The Jam Band name had had its day and that, to reflect the new outlook – and the fact that someone like Steven Tallarico didn't just join someone else's group – a new name had to be found.

That particular move was held in abeyance as a far more substantial change took place. Now was the time to take things seriously, to graft Tallarico's relentless professionalism onto the boisterousness of the others. With Perry and Hamilton living in Sunapee, and Tallarico and Tabano based in New York, something had to give. The four chose to move to Boston where Tabano owned a clothing store selling leather goods. Still short of a drummer, Tabano opened the doors of his store one day to encounter Joey Kramer, a kid who'd also been to Roosevelt High back in Yonkers with him and Tallarico. Sharing an equally impressive disciplinary record – he'd been thrown out three times for fighting – Kramer had heard that Tabano's band were on the look-out for a drummer. He auditioned the same day and got the job.

One problem loomed for Kramer. He was enrolled at the Berkeley School of Music where he was studying theory and composition. Should he leave school for a band with no name? Eventually, it was the fact that Tallarico was involved that convinced him to join the others. Like Hamilton and Perry before him, he recognised Steven's star quality. Tallarico inspired the conviction that he was going to make it big, and that going along with him for the ride would be a lot of fun. Kramer quit after two terms, telling his distraught parents, 'I thought I'd learn more out in front of people playing every night.'

It was fortunate that Kramer came on board, for not only did it release Steven from his percussive chores, it provided the group with their name – Aerosmith. Kramer had spent his schooldays doodling disinterestedly, and that name was the one that he regularly came back to, writing it again and again, thinking it would be great name for a rock band. His new colleagues agreed, and Aerosmith was born. If nothing else, it was a hell of an improvement on their original idea, The Hookers, though maybe that might have been more appropriate for the defiantly sexual shapes thrown by Tallarico. Rescued from the drum-stool, he was a revelation, a swaggering, innovative and compulsively watchable front-man. From the outset of any Aerosmith gig, the audience couldn't drag their eyes away from this incredible egomaniac who could outstrut even the mighty Jagger, then at his peak. In the small venues Aerosmith played at this early stage of their career, Steven was just too damned big for the stage, a personality that overwhelmed everything in its path. Paradoxically, in the clubs and schools that they played Tallarico was almost an Achilles heel, for his broad brush act didn't work so well in those confined spaces. Here was a man destined to hold vast stadiums in the palm of his hand, but face-to-face on a tiny stage, he was overbearing.

Nevertheless, Aerosmith had begun to make progress holed up in their Boston home. Flat broke, they had to share a seven-room apartment on Commonwealth Avenue where Perry recalls them eating nothing but 'jelly sandwiches and Campbell's soup for a whole year' right through 1970. As part of their career strategy, they played comparatively few gigs during this period, a tactic Tallarico sold to the others. Instead of playing live, they would rehearse, rehearse, rehearse, playing rock standards as well as the new, original material for which Steven was largely responsible. Kramer later pointed out, 'We never wanted to get stuck in the clubs, we wanted to be a concert group, play on a bigger stage all over the country, all over the world. We were ambitious.'

By denying themselves live work in this way, they were also denying themselves a source of income, so they took a variety of small-time jobs to bring in some cash. Steven, for instance, worked briefly in a bakery, while more bizarrely, Joe worked as a caretaker in a synagogue. The evenings were spent in getting communally stoned and playing Deep Purple's *Machine Head* and Jeff Beck's *Rough And Ready* into the ground, making it obvious where their pile-driving power came from. However, so authentic was their early blues-based material that they must have cast their net much further than that.

Gigs were played occasionally, the first taking place at Nipmuc Regional High School. Tom Hamilton recalls the gig mainly by reference to 'a real big fight between Steven and Joe about Joe playing too loud – so began an Aerosmith tradition!' Their set included 'Shapes Of Things' by The Yardbirds, 'Live With Me' by the inevitable Rolling Stones and Lennon's epic 'Cold Turkey'. In fact, though people were to harp on with the Stones comparisons right through Aerosmith's first decade, they were often a lot closer to late-period Beatles circa *Abbey Road* and Lennon's seminal *John Lennon/Plastic Ono Band* album. Certainly their strong sense of dark instrumental chaos and a brooding musical menace allied to a sure grasp of melody sounded like it had come in through the bathroom window.

High schools remained their venue of choice, and they would also venture out to play The Weekly Boogie at Boston University. Indeed, on occasion, they'd even just set up their gear outside the university and play a set on the spot. This erratic working schedule enabled them to devote more time to practising than almost any of their contemporaries. They responded with a frightening devotion to the work ethic, playing hard in rehearsals, constantly fine-tuning every aspect of their act. Though Perry and Tallarico came from diametrically opposed points of the spectrum when it came to arrangements – Steven wanted them tight, Joe didn't – they endured this potentially explosive period by virtue of their burgeoning friendship. Steven noted, 'Joe was a guy I could sit down and make patty cakes with, like your mom brings you over and within minutes you're playing and you're compatible.' Given their competitive natures, it was only friendship that held Aerosmith together for so long in what were to become astonishingly fractious times.

Their rigorous rehearsal schedule made it clear that Ray Tabano wasn't going to fit into the band as well as they'd hoped. Although he'd played with them in a few high-profile shows at New York's Academy of Music, where they had opened for Humble Pie and Edgar Winter, there was no real interaction taking place between him and Perry. The necessary emotional contact between the two just wasn't there, so they couldn't play off one another and consequently the music was falling flat. With the sparks already flying between Tallarico and Perry, it was essential that Perry should be pushed and pulled instrumentally too, while at the same time being offered a reliable safety net by a solid rhythm guitarist. Ultimately, Tabano sold up and moved to Mexico, returning to the fold later on as stage manager. He was replaced as rhythm guitarist by Brad Whitford, who though originally from Winchester in Massachusetts, was now another New Yorker. He had previously played with the band Justin Thyme, and having known Perry since they were thirteen, the two quickly built up a common musical language.

Aerosmith were transformed into a tougher unit almost immediately and their increased confidence was reflected in their decision to increase their workload, playing more and more clubs in the Boston area, occasionally travelling further afield. Nevertheless, schools remained their staple source of income, not least because often they paid better than the clubs. Tom Hamilton recalls the period vividly, pointing out, 'We played damned near every high school in Boston and New Hampshire. We'd set up and play for fifty people, anybody who'd listen.'

Aerosmith were also playing the odd show in New York too, much to Steven's delight. The great showman was pleased to discover that his band – and he'd begun to think of Aerosmith as his band – were able to hold a crowd's attention. 'When we started, I imagined people like Rick Derringer were like Lord High Doodledums who sat in the corner with servants picking their toes. But we played Max's in New York with those guys, and I knew we had more than they had.'

Some of Tallarico's comments were born out of bravado but there was also a grain of truth in his assessments. American rock music was relatively banal at the time with much of FM radio's output being soporific in the extreme. By 1970, the Beatles and The Yardbirds were gone, but the most aggressive and exciting music still tended to come out of Britain. Replacing their predecessors, Led Zeppelin,

Deep Purple and Black Sabbath were making inroads into the lucrative US market, showing the home-grown competition to be worthless, pale imitations in the process. The multi-platinum selling singer and guitarist Rick Derringer, for example, pedalled rock at its softest and had all the personality of a cornflake, while the few American talents worthy of real consideration, such as the eccentric genius Todd Rundgren, were often regarded as being just too odd for mainstream consumption. In short, Americans had a seemingly insatiable appetite for hard-edged, straightforward rock, but there was no one besides the British interlopers that could give it to them. That's where Aerosmith were looking to come in. Perry and Whitford provided the right blend on guitar, and Tallarico had as much star quality as any band could handle. When you added the fact that, when sharing the microphone, Joe and Steven looked uncannily like Mick 'n' Keef, you have a group that looked unstoppable.

This fact quickly became apparent to Bostonian promoter Frank Connelly. He'd been alerted to their promise by John O'Toole, a friend who ran The Fenway Theater and who'd been letting Aerosmith rehearse there. Connelly took over their management almost immediately, persuading them that they needed to play live on a more regular basis. He moved them out of Commonwealth Avenue and put them in The Manchester Sheraton Hotel in Boston where they continued to work intensively. This put a terrible strain on the fledgling band, notably the relationship between Kramer and the man he had replaced on drums, Tallarico. As a former drummer and the main songwriter, Steven had very fixed ideas on the way the songs should sound and he drove Joey to distraction making him play things time and again until they'd been played to his satisfaction. Having worked in a much looser environment as a soul drummer prior to hooking up with Aerosmith, this discipline was new to Joey and he found it tough to cope with. After several more months of this back-breaking, balls-aching refinement, both Connelly and, maybe more importantly, Tallarico pronounced Aerosmith ready to record. They put together a selection of their best material, recording a demo tape in Boston. Connelly was then assiduous in his attempts to rustle up music industry interest, but, as a purely local figure, he knew he lacked the big punch when it came to mixing it with the New York and Los Angeles heavyweights who would ultimately make or break the band.

Acting admirably and wholly in the interests of his charges, Connelly approached the Leber-Krebs management organisation. They took over the running of Aerosmith in return for a co-management credit for Connelly on their first two records and a slice of their publishing over the same period. This was still a lucrative deal, but there's little doubt that he could have done much better for himself by holding on to Aerosmith, even if in doing so he might have held back their career. Connelly was soon to be stricken with cancer and 1982's *Rock In A Hard Place* was dedicated to him, a tribute to one who had played a small yet absolutely crucial role in the story.

The change in management worked in the band's favour within a matter of weeks. Early in 1972, they made the most of their contacts and so a copy of Aerosmith's demo was placed on the desk of Columbia's President, Clive Davis. Having heard their potential in its rawest state, Davis decided to see if they could play live. At Max's Kansas City in New York, he decided that Aerosmith offered too good an opportunity to be missed, even though representatives from Atlantic Records attended the same show and decided they'd pass. Steven remembered, 'Before some summer gig at a high school somewhere, David Krebs arrived with this big wad, maybe a thousand dollars, and we'd signed to CBS [Columbia was a subsidiary label].'

The original contract was for $125,000, requiring the band to deliver two albums a year. Fortunately, that last part was negotiable for they were never to threaten such regularity at any time. What wasn't negotiable was the fact that, thoroughly naive in business matters, Aerosmith had actually signed with Leber-Krebs. It was Leber-Krebs who were effectively signed to Columbia, their relationship locked in by a production contract. Aerosmith had signed away their own freedom, seduced by a thousand bucks and a promise.

Leber-Krebs knew the music business inside out and were among the shrewdest of operators, though even they had had their failures. Like all successful businessmen, they'd written those mistakes off to experience and had learned the appropriate lessons, something which

21

was to benefit Aerosmith. Leber-Krebs had been the management company behind The New York Dolls, the prototype punks who seemed destined to be America's biggest and best band of the 1970s, but who fell apart by 1974 without ever having fulfilled their glorious promise. David Krebs admitted, 'The Dolls made the mistake of getting too heavily into the unisex trip,' which had confused middle America. This let-down was an important part of Leber-Krebs managerial education though, and it helped them steer Tallarico away from a similarly mistaken path, Steven, 'having the good sense to go in the direction of The Rolling Stones of the 1970s, which was more sexually ambiguous and so much more difficult to pin down.'

Another problem which beset the Dolls was the incredible hype that surrounded them. The fire, fed unmercifully by both Leber-Krebs and their record company Mercury, eventually engulfed the band, who could never deliver what was promised – The New York Dolls were different, certainly, but they weren't the revolutionary rebirth of rock 'n' roll that they were alleged to be by the promotional material. Trying to live up to these claims, the Dolls simply fell apart. Wisely, no such extravagant claims were ever made for Aerosmith, and Leber-Krebs set about marketing them as America's greatest old-fashioned, good-time rock 'n' roll band, exciting followers in the great British tradition. What you saw was what you got, a line that made perfect sense for Aerosmith, the ultimate party band. Sadly, those parties would soon get out of hand.

3

MAKIN' IT

An up-and-coming band spends its youthful energy in the sole pursuit of that precious piece of paper that represents a recording contract. When they've got it, there's a strong temptation to think that they've made it. In truth, the deal is just the beginning of the real hard work. A contract isn't an end in itself, but merely a means towards achieving an artist's ambitions. Aerosmith, especially Tallarico, wanted to dominate the American music scene, to become the biggest stars in the country. Steven was quick to appreciate the subtle change in their way of life and was happy to do all that was necessary to break the band, even if that included changing his name. Officially, Tallarico was thought to be too awkward a name for a thrusting rock star to be encumbered with so, legend has it, he picked the name Tyler out of a hat. Steven Tyler rolled off the tongue a little easier, but it also distanced the singer from any ethnic connotations and his Italian background. Maybe their label or the management felt that an all-American band should be just that, without any reference to other cultures – the same logic was certainly followed a decade later when Jon Bongiovi became Jon Bon Jovi.

Whatever the case, Aerosmith now had a record as well as their name to make. Tyler's endless devotion to writing and rehearsing had left the band in a very good position going in to the recording. Instead of working on the live circuit where so many bands became sloppy, Aerosmith had songs and arrangements that were watertight. If other bands might ruin their songs by playing them in too many couldn't-care-less-bars, Aerosmith's songs were enlivened by the comparatively few times they'd been aired live. Even so, live work began to take up an increasing amount of their time as they began to play regularly across the East coast of America, attempting to build up some kind of fan-base in anticipation of the début record.

With Columbia looking for a release in January 1973, the band began working at Boston's Intermedia Sound studio, under the guidance of Adrian Barber, selected as producer following his work with Cream and Vanilla Fudge, bands who had been the inspiration behind The Jam Band. Columbia didn't want to risk too much cash on an unproven rock 'n' roll band at a time when fashions in music were tending towards the complexities offered by Yes, Pink Floyd and Emerson, Lake And Palmer. If Columbia wanted to keep the budget down, Intermedia was the place to do it for, even by 1972 standards, the equipment there was primitive. That showed through on the album too, for the eponymous *Aerosmith* does sound ramshackle to say the least, with none of the clarity that Perry's guitar lines required. As such, the album proved to be disappointing, especially in retrospect, yet there was still much to enjoy from both performance and songwriting. Indeed, years later, reviewing a CD reissue, *Q*'s David Cavanagh was able to describe it as 'fresh and cocky', *Vox*'s Stephen Dalton calling it 'lean and flouncy'. There were very few frills on the album, that was for sure.

Tyler was, inevitably, the star of the show, flexing his musical muscles and making it very clear to all that as far as he was concerned, Steven Tyler called the shots in Aerosmith. Ironically though, it was as a writer rather than performer that he stood out, for the mix was so cloudy that vocally he seemed wholly unremarkable. However, he contributed to seven of the eight songs that made up the album, the exception being the old blues chestnut 'Walkin' The Dog', which finished the album in excellent fashion. That was extremely important for they had endured a very faltering start, with 'Makin' It' and 'Somebody' having little to commend them. The former was standard 1970s rock 'n' roll, rather pedestrian if anything and with no spark of originality, while the latter was solid bluesy hard rock of the kind you might find on any Deep Purple album, but done far better.

Aerosmith got its kick-start with the third number, 'Dream On', which has been described as the band's own 'Stairway To Heaven'. While not as epochal as that song, it did have Led Zeppelin influences, with Tyler's voice being very similar to Robert Plant's in many places. 'Dream On' had a more considered, intelligent and interesting lyric, even if it flirted with cliché at times. Its anthemic character was crucial in Aerosmith's search for their own sense of identity, while the restraint of the playing was impressive – the delicacy of such a ballad could very easily have been swamped by epic instrumentation.

It was as if 'Dream On' had flooded the band with confidence, for the rest of the album was so much more impressive than its lacklustre start had promised. 'One Way Street' leant heavily on their influences, notably the Stones and the Yardbirds. Playing the white man's blues, the band sounded increasingly at home, and Tyler responded with a more distinctive vocal performance which suggested that in time he would wrestle free of his influences and become his own man. 'Mama Kin' reinforced that impression, Tyler having the title tattooed on his arm such was his love for his song, which he felt would become 'legendary'. Never one to sell himself short with false modesty, this time Tyler's ample faith in his own talent was justified as they produced a derivative but very exciting track that was elevated by some beautiful guitar work from Joe Perry, his best on the album.

'Write Me' followed, allowing some brief relaxation with an archetypal Stonesy blow-out, but again Tyler demonstrated his grasp of melody by injecting a Beatles' feel to proceedings.

If Aerosmith had chosen to go in a different direction after this album came out, their reputation as authentic bluesmen would have been made by the last two songs. The first was 'Movin' Out', the first Perry/Tyler collaboration and a hugely promising one, a rootsy romp, redolent of the delta. Lyrically it dabbled in the 'cosmic' style that was so fashionable and which has dated badly, but that aside, the song has held up well. Perry and Whitford worked off one another splendidly and Tyler's voice continued to develop, putting his own stamp on the song, finding a voice, covering it with his own personality. The quality of 'Movin' Out' is emphasised by the fact that it doesn't suffer in comparison with 'Walkin' The Dog', which follows it. Although they sound more at home playing this than some of their own material, it reinforced the opinion that Aerosmith had a genuine feeling for the blues and that they should mine that seam rather than experimenting with forms with which they were less comfortable. Aerosmith were clearly a blues group and not a progressive rock band. Unfortunately, someone at Columbia failed to recognise this and saddled the album with a dismal sleeve, a fey, ethereal, up-in-the-clouds concept presumably inspired by the 'aero' of their name. It suggested that Aerosmith were a bunch of drippy hippies and did their profile and image as hard rockers no good at all.

Nonetheless, given all the financial restrictions under which the album was recorded, it was a sturdy début effort that showcased a tight if nervous group, and promised more than it delivered. At the very least, it provided ample illustration that here was a band that Columbia could profitably support, especially as the most striking thing about Aerosmith was the group's attitude. Even though it was obvious that neither he nor the band were the finished article, Tyler's performance seemed to say, 'Aren't we what you've all been waiting for?'

Columbia's president Clive Davis was enthusiastic and the omens were good in the first weeks following release – the album grazed the *Billboard* chart at number 166 on issue, respectable enough for an unknown act.

Sadly, just as their momentum was beginning to build, in the summer of 1973, Columbia was rocked by a scandal which culminated in Davis's dismissal in July when his position became untenable beneath the weight of payola and heroin trafficking allegations. What was a personal tragedy for the high-flying Davis was a professional disaster for Aerosmith. Davis had been their friend in the highest of places, but once he'd departed, Columbia's executives were happy to milk the cash cows that were Chicago and Barbra Streisand to the detriment of the rest of the roster. Aerosmith found themselves all but ignored.

There was only one solution available to them. They had to go out on the road with a vengeance and find their own audience without the aid of the record company. They continued to be successful in New

Hampshire and Boston, the groundwork they'd done over the previous couple of years standing them in good stead. Indeed, it was impressive sales in those catchment areas that had propelled Aerosmith towards the lower regions of the chart – without those fans even number 166 would have been beyond them. Elsewhere, as Joe Perry conceded, 'We did lousy for a while.' Columbia had little idea of how to promote them and it was especially dispiriting when 'Dream On' was half-heartedly released as a single in December of 1973. Despite an utter lack of any kind of promotion, the single managed to reach number fifty-nine, showing that with the right push, Aerosmith could become a real force. Instead, Columbia took it as a sign that Aerosmith were going nowhere fast and left them to their own devices.

Those devices were purely road-based. 'Dream On' had given them a calling card of sorts which enabled them to break out of the East coast ghetto they'd been operating in, allowing them to see the rest of America. Joe recalled, 'The thing that really started to turn it around for us was the first "Dream On" release as a single. Then things slowly started to pick up, we came out of New England and started to move.' The management's philosophy was simple – let the people see the band and make up their own minds.

Mention has already been made of the way The New York Dolls faltered beneath the weight of unfair expectations, built in part by Leber-Krebs. For Aerosmith, expectations were, if anything, damped down. You didn't go to an Aerosmith show expecting to see the future of rock 'n' roll. You went to see a bunch of ordinary guys with a flamboyant front-man rocking up a storm and giving you a good time. They didn't want to change the world, they didn't want to change your life, they didn't want to laugh at all the bands that had gone before, they just wanted to make you feel good about things for an hour or two. That was what was promised, that was what they could deliver. With that in mind, support slots became a regular staple of band life. Some were highly successful, others less so, with Krebs admitting to the odd major mismatch, 'I let my booking agent talk me into having them open for the Mahavishnu Orchestra, which was a definite minus. But we learned to play our market so that Aerosmith opened for acts that were slightly on the downside – bands whose audience we could cop. Even if we didn't blow them off the stage every time, we could at least count on some to buy an Aerosmith album.'

Supports with The Kinks and Mott the Hoople were ideal for there was some musical similarity; while Aerosmith were on the way up The Kinks, in particular, were on the way out. Aerosmith regularly blew them off-stage, Tyler was in his element and the band was mopping up new fans by the score. The problem was that this was a drip-drip effect rather than a torrential outpouring of new support, so back at Columbia few realised that they had a growing band on their hands.

Musically, the live toughening-up process was having a beneficial effect on the group. Perry and Whitford were increasingly powerful, Tyler's growth in confidence meant he became more and more relaxed as a performer, and the rhythm section of Kramer and Hamilton were as impressive a pairing as any hard rock band had a right to be, Kramer's soul roots infiltrating the music. But spending day after day on the road without a break was already beginning to take its toll. 'Mama Kin' had already hinted at the frenetic lifestyle they'd endured prior to signing with Columbia. That was nothing compared with the schedule Aerosmith had to look forward to now. Pretty quickly, the excitement started to wear off and they began to balk at the treadmill they were locked on to. Recreations beyond the purely musical were becoming increasingly important to relieve the tensions that they all felt. Early on, the crushing boredom of life on the road was offset by the escape routes offered in an endless whirl of parties and clubs and a constant flow of drinks, girls and pharmaceuticals.

In the 1970s drugs had increasingly become widely available and the image of the rock musician smoking and snorting as much and as many varieties of drugs as he could lay his hands on grew. Not only was it exciting but some also suggested that experimenting with drugs helped foster creativity. Drink was always on hand too, generally in enormous quantities. It might have seemed like a dream come true to be a rock star with any number of hangers-on appearing at your elbow to supply your every need; but in the long term it was to have awful implications, with many falling victim to the pernicious lifestyle.

For the insecure Tyler in particular, such freedom was dangerous. Covering his uncertainty with a raucous bravado, he was always vulnerable to the need to conform to the rock star stereotype, and then to take that to its illogical conclusion. Thinking back later, he said, 'I grew up with a John Wayne mentality. If you were a two-fisted drinker, you were cool. I wanted to be cool. Then I wanted to be cooler. As a kid in the Bronx where I grew up, I was this goofy, white, big-lipped, jerky looking kid. I wanted to be cool and so I eventually turned into a flaming alcoholic.' With a raging taste for alcohol already well developed, it was unsurprising that as soon as he started to get it for free, Tyler took all that he could get.

To make matters worse, Steven wasn't the kind of guy who could stop when he'd had enough, simply because he never felt he had had enough. 'I'm an addictive personality. I'm high-strung and impatient. I've got to have everything yesterday. I've got all this nervous energy that I've got to get rid of. Drugs and booze seemed to help me cope. In the 1970s it was cool to do drugs. If you could go to a party, have a girl on your arm and do all the drugs in the place you were cool.'

Essentially, the things that made Tyler an exceptional front-man were also the seeds of his eventual near self-destruction. That nervous energy fuelled his stage performances. That addictive nature drove him to get the songs right when others might have left them only partly formed. His impatience for success pushed Aerosmith on, keeping them out on the road when they might have been better advised to rest. Of course, the pressures that built up on the road only added to Tyler's problems, fraying his nerves, winding him up yet further to the point of nervous exhaustion. Yet such were the demands on him and the band, he couldn't bow down to tiredness, and so he needed further stimulants to keep him going. For the next decade Steven Tyler was locked into a vicious circle that he was lucky to survive. The signs were already there in 1973, particularly on the artwork of the second album, where the normally gaunt Tyler is clearly bloated around the face, the drink taking its toll on his physical appearance. It hadn't got to the music yet, though . . .

4

ROUND AND ROUND . . . AND ROUND

Aerosmith accepted that they were approaching crunch time when they got down to work on their second album which went under the working title of *A Night In The Ruts*. With Columbia's attitude to them being indifferent at best, they were lucky to grab the services of Jack Douglas as producer. Adrian Barber had helped educate them in the ways of the studio, but the stakes were too high now to allow the music to suffer from the inadequacies of the début. Douglas was equally keen to make his mark as a top-quality producer, having worked mainly as an engineer in the past, including stints alongside the album's executive producer Bob Ezrin. Their work on Alice Cooper's records has been suggested as having been the template for this second Aerosmith opus, but that's far too simplistic a view. If anything, the inspiration for some sections of the record was John Lennon, and it was here that Douglas was in his element. His feel for hard rock was never in doubt but his own devotion to Lennon indicated that he was a man who could see beyond its narrow confines. Working alongside the group, they hoped that he might be able to encourage their more melodic instincts which had lain largely dormant on that début record. Basically, rather than Alice, they were looking at the sound that Lennon employed on solo records such as *Some Time In New York City*, his work with Elephant's Memory being especially influential – 'Pandora's Box', the album's final track with its pumping horn section a case in point.

Get Your Wings, as the album was finally titled, represented a quantum leap from the diffidence of the début. They sounded like a band that knew America would fall under their spell. Bold, brassy, cocky in the extreme, Aerosmith took no prisoners this time around. Joe Perry launched his claim to Keith Richards' throne as the human riff right from the outset on 'Same Old Song And Dance', the use of horns adding a new dimension to the sound. Deft touches in the arrangements abounded over the course of the album and it was obvious that Douglas had had an influence. Working at New York's Record Plant facility, Aerosmith were greeted with state-of-the-art equipment and used it to the full, capturing a wider sonic picture than had been possible at Intermedia, with Perry benefiting commensurately. He shone again on his other co-composition, 'Spaced', where his impressive lead work managed to overshadow some dismal sub-sci-fi lyrics. Small wonder that Guns N' Roses were to laud Aerosmith more than a decade later as the instrumentation on songs like 'Spaced' provided them with their blueprint.

As Guns N' Roses learned from Aerosmith, so Aerosmith had borrowed from the Stones. 'Lord Of The Thighs' was a highly significant song for the band in many ways. Steven's piano playing was a delight, even if it was a direct take from 'Have You Seen Your Mother Baby', but more importantly it marked the first appearance of Tyler in his role as the lecher, his vocals dripping with contempt and predatory venom. As raunchy a cut as you could wish to hear, it marked the direction that Tyler would take throughout his career, though later he would be rather more subtle in his use of innuendo and the double entendre. This new character was reinforced on 'Pandora's Box' when references such as 'spreads like Flora' and 'slitty licker' were vulgarly unambiguous in the extreme, lacking in the wit that characterised later records. 'Pandora's Box', which brought down the curtain on the album, made it very clear that Steven Tyler had also finally found his own voice. There had been occasional lapses into Robert Plantisms, notably on 'Woman Of The World' but, by and large, Tyler had allowed himself to be himself. This was utterly crucial to Aerosmith's development, for he evolved a unique style.

The rhythmic piano playing on 'Lord Of The Thighs' had been a pertinent reminder of Tyler's earlier career as a drummer, and now

31

he began to sing in the same fashion. Rather than screaming the words out like most hard rock chest-beaters were wont to do, Tyler spat out his vocals like a character from a Damon Runyon story. Streetwise, sharp-talking, hard as nails, the staccato delivery augmented Aerosmith's aggressively macho stance and was absolutely made to complement Perry's guitar playing. Joe was often taking the melody lines that would normally have been the preserve of the singer, Tyler filling in additional rhythm in the same style that rap artists have made their own in recent years. What that meant was that not only were Aerosmith a great hard rock act, they were a brilliant dance band too.

In the wake of 'Dream On', Tyler had attempted to pen another winning ballad with the atmospheric 'Seasons Of Wither'. Zeppelinesque again, Perry's guitar reminiscent of Jimmy Page, the song was played with an effortless yet very precise power, even though its rather crass, yearning mysticism left it moored in rock cliché. More satisfactory was 'Train Kept A Rollin'', their reading of which owed a great deal to The Yardbirds' version. *Rolling Stone*'s Charley Walters pointed out that, 'They've absorbed yet varied the styles of their mentors, creating their own in the process. They think 1966 and play 1974, something which a lot of groups would like to boast.'

With *Get Your Wings* unleashed in early 1974 – it didn't get a British release until October of that year – its eventual *Billboard* listing at number seventy-four represented a healthy if unspectacular growth in popularity. That popularity was hard earned on the back of a tireless schedule, one they intended to maintain. As soon as the album was completed, Aerosmith were back in the old routine, touring America remorselessly on their own and, more regularly, as the opening act in some of America's biggest arenas. The next eighteen months saw the band work themselves into an absolute frenzy, never pausing for breath. Tyler, still a small-time rocker in national terms, was already beginning to earn himself a reputation for his astonishing intake of drink and drugs. Early in 1975, he proudly confessed, 'I'm an alkie from the start. Wake up and have a beer with my Rice Krispies.'

In turn, the rest of the band indulged themselves to the maximum.

Of them all, it was probably Joe Perry who was the worst affected, for it was he who felt he had to compete with Tyler's prodigious consumption of booze. This was yet another example of the way Aerosmith's success would inevitably lead to their demise for he and Tyler were incredibly competitive with one another. Their musical partnership was at the heart of the group in and out of the studio, and it was because they were so determined to outdo one another that many of their best songs were written. If Perry created the main riff for 'Same Old Song And Dance', Tyler would have to respond with 'Lord Of The Thighs'.

Initially this was wholly healthy, pushing them on to greater and greater things. Indeed, had the two not been so competitive, then for all their ability Aerosmith might never had made it out of the clubs. Each man wanted to write a better song than the other, a bigger hit, play or sing louder than the other, get more fans, more groupies. This had to spill over into their drinking too. If Joe had a big glass of Jack in his hand, Steven had to have two. If Steven had got his hands on some cocaine, Joe needed to respond in kind with a bigger stash. Their salvation was their relative youth – Tyler, the oldest, was just twenty-six and courtesy of the effort he put into the stage show, as fit as could be – and that they were still a support act. Travelling in reasonable style and comfort courtesy of the headliners, they had decent dressing-rooms, were secure in the knowledge that the dope they took was good stuff, and then they only had to play a twenty-five minute set. Even under the influence, twenty-five minutes was a breeze for troopers like Tyler and Perry. In fact it was the ideal length of time for them to work off the early-evening booze and work up an appetite for a good night out.

To be fair, the band were acting in the way that any bunch of healthy young men might when confronted by the alluring temptations of girls, drinks and drugs. Some would say that they were merely revelling in the spirit of the times. Joe Perry pointed out, 'Whatever I was doing around the business in the 1970s, I'd be doing blow and everyone with me would be doing the same. And if they weren't, it was them that had the problem, not me.' It seemed to them that everyone was living life to the full in those pre-AIDS, pre-crack days. So you drank, so what? So you worked your way through a high school's worth of girls? Perk of the job. So you smoked a bit, snorted a little. It made you a better musician, didn't it?

Life as a support band gave Aerosmith the opportunity to experience the rock 'n' roll lifestyle, but it was just a provisional licence. The year that they finally passed their test was 1975. Looking ahead to their third album, they'd been able to set aside a little more time for writing and recording. With two flops behind them, it wasn't inconceivable that Columbia would drop them if the third album didn't make it and, given the way Columbia were promoting them, or rather, not promoting them, it began to look as though they were viewing Aerosmith as nothing more than a tax loss. It was doubly frustrating because the band knew that the reaction on the ground was improving all the time and that there was an audience ready and waiting to be taken. Support slots with Deep Purple, Black Sabbath – reflected in the heavyweight new song 'Round And Round' – and ZZ Top had proved to them that there were people out there who wanted to hear the music but who often couldn't find their records in the racks.

The first indication that their work was paying off came in July when a lead-off single, 'Sweet Emotion', gave them their first top forty hit. They had to capitalise on that and with *Toys In The Attic*, they had the perfect vehicle, their first 100% classic album and one which would go down in history as a seminal blast of hard rock 'n' roll; many devotees still feel that the album represents their finest hour. Undoubtedly it was potent evidence that all the hard road-work was bearing fruit. After a couple of albums that had been enjoyable but largely derivative, Aerosmith had found their own groove at last, described later by *Q*'s David Cavanagh as 'Fat, syncopated riffs and Aerosmith's big trick – sneering, whining, slightly psychedelic harmonies led by Tyler's panicky, fag-ash voice.' Whatever the ups and downs they were to endure in the coming years, no one would ever again be able to deny that Aerosmith had their own distinctive and instantly recognisable sound, which they have since exploited to the nth degree.

Toys In The Attic gave the band their first gold record, quickly racking up 500,000 sales, charting at number eleven and dragging both its predecessors towards gold status in its wake. Success was well deserved too, for from the fierce aggression of the title track through to the melodrama of the closing ballad 'You See Me Crying', Aerosmith were firing on all cylinders and showcasing a versatility that few had imagined they might possess. Surprisingly, early reviewers were restrained, wondering if they might have missed the boat again. *Rolling Stone*'s Gordon Fletcher pointed out that hitherto, they were a band of 'almost unlimited potential [that] can't seem to hurdle the last boulder separating it from commercial success.' Fletcher went on to criticise the record's production values, decrying, 'A more compact, jumbled mix that gives more of a group feel but robs them of that explosive ambience. Hence its much harder to get involved with the music at first exposure to it.'

That was a peculiar observation, for few records have opened with the dramatic punch of *Toys In The Attic*, the title song hurtling along with a focused, purposeful aggression that outdid anything they'd recorded previously. If in the past their hard edge had been blunted, this time they were playing with a passion that did justice to their show. Jack Douglas deserved credit for that as *Sounds*' Jonh Ingham agreed, opining, 'They do carry off their Anglo pretensions with some class, but the most important person on the disc is producer Jack Douglas who can take the worst rockaboogie muzak the band deliver and inject some hooks and touches that make the ears perk up.'

A little harsh on Aerosmith's writing perhaps, for they had their strongest body of work thus far to show, but Douglas was becoming an integral part of the team. Part of his strength was in helping opposing ideas to rub against one another, each gaining in impact by virtue of the contrast. For a record that was so musically positive, the lyrical sentiments were a lot more downbeat. 'Toys' itself was an example, acting as a rites of passage opus, following the band members from teenage years on to a lifestyle where there was no chance to take a breath. The way in which they'd become divorced from ordinary life was reinforced by lines that spoke of leaving real things behind. It was a theme that characterised the whole record, the strongest hints so far that life in a band wasn't the glamorous dream it was supposed to be. 'Round And Round', powered by a heavy Sabbath-like undertow made further mention of the 'road warp' that was beginning to afflict them, with its themes of betrayal and of complete confusion, the singer unable to recall his own name.

The theme of spiralling out of control was developed further on 'No More No More', a brilliant Tyler/Perry collaboration. Revelling in the songs of their youth, this was a real Stonesy singalong with an Aerosmith twist. The atmosphere went the full nine yards, creating a powerful image of the group playing live, swigging bottles of beer, smoking Marlboros, flowing scarves all over the place, yet it wasn't all fun – as Tyler said, 'We signed to Columbia, and we thought, 'Man, this is it! Aerosmith has arrived!" Three years on, I still ain't seen daylight since I started this band.' The title refrain made it obvious that both the workload and the accoutrements that went with success – girls, bad reviews, booze, the clap – could be too much, but it also made it apparent that rock 'n' roll was still a pretty cool way of making a living, and that despite everything, its allure remained. Tyler was married to the band, not to any of the ladies who passed through his life. Nowadays, that sounds hopelessly dumb, yet at the time, it was the prevailing attitude, and few eyebrows were raised at this macho, sexist posturing.

'Sweet Emotion' attempted to put a different slant on things, arguing that so fast were things moving, it was impossible for Tyler and his colleagues to say just where they'd be in a year, so how could they hope to settle down? Musically 'Sweet Emotion' was one of their more adventurous departures to date, featuring an hypnotic groove and seductive vocal, enhanced by a bone-crunching Page-like riff. The Zeppelin references were much more apparent on this album than on either of those that had gone before. It's tempting therefore to consider whether Aerosmith were deliberately moving in that direction so that they could fill the void that Zeppelin left during their regular periods off the road. By 1975, Zeppelin were probably the world's greatest concert draw and consequently, they were starting to rein in the frequency of their appearances, no longer needing to chase the dollar. Joe Perry was candid enough to accept that, 'We made it because we were the guys you could actually see. It wasn't like Zeppelin was out on the road all the time. The Stones weren't always coming to your town. But every eight or nine months, there we were. We were America's band – the garage band that made it real big, the party band.'

Finally, Perry's ambition to play white blues through huge Marshall stacks and pack halls across America was coming to fruition. Having attacked that strategy with single-minded dedication, the rewards were waiting for them. The relaxed warmth and good humour of much of *Toys In The Attic* made it apparent that they knew their time had come. If they hadn't had such self-belief, they would never have dared record Fred Weismantel's 'Big Ten Inch Record', a colourful jazz/blues shuffle that was a wonderful choice of cover. Dripping in the sort of witty innuendo and comic timing that Tyler himself had been looking to emulate, this twenty-year-old tune summed up Aerosmith's lighter side, emphasising that they were there to give everyone a helluva good time. Tyler was beginning to get it right too, as he proved on 'Adam's Apple' where his attempts at humour were less leaden than before. On a different tack, with 'You See Me Crying' he acquitted himself well in a mournful, self-pitying tone, a collaboration with Chain Reaction partner Don Solomon in the Nilsson/Elton John vein. A confused, bittersweet ballad, it was all the more affecting for its juxtaposition with 'Round And Round'.

The remaining two tracks were very different, indicating that the band were branching out and thinking more deeply about their records. 'Uncle Salty' was constructed around a relaxed, laid-back groove and featured delightful vocal harmonies copped from The Beatles. Effectively employing the contrasts again, this cool, sunny music backed a tale of child abuse and descent into drugs and prostitution, marred only by some of Tyler's less sensitive puns. Nevertheless, tackling such an issue in 1975 was particularly brave, though few observers picked up on it at the time, presumably not wishing to court the controversy that surrounded such a taboo subject.

'Walk This Way', a jokey tale of lost virginity, was adorned by one of the great rock guitar riffs, a huge fat, funky, in your face blast from Perry who, with his inspirational playing on this album, had established himself on a level alongside many of his great heroes. Keith Richards or Jeff Beck would have loved to have written 'Walk This Way', and Perry could have hoped for few finer compliments.

Even so, *Rolling Stone* weren't thrilled, the review concluding with a backhanded compliment to the effect that, 'If they return to the production that made *Get Your Wings* so memorable, and if they avoid tepid, trite material, their potential is extremely high.' *Sounds* was a little kinder, if more convoluted in its assessment: 'On one hand the baseball bat and sledgehammer syndrome and on the other pretensions to rock art. All raging guitars, quaint lyrics and echoed harmony choruses against vibrant riffing, one could be excused for categorising them as an American Queen [but] the illusion disappears under encroaching ethnicism . . . not unlike sitting under the Golden Arches munching a McDonald's burger while grooving on some Aubrey Beardsley prints. Which ain't bad at all as long as you don't spill ketchup on the pages.' In time *Toys In The Attic* received the plaudits it deserved, *Q*'s Mat Snow delivering this more measured view in 1991: 'Piston-hipped brawn and devil-may-care brain delivers in full measure the promise of the band's gun-slinging attitood.'

With its excellent chart placing, *Toys In The Attic* had dispelled many of the doubts that had continued to hover around Aerosmith, although Columbia remained unconvinced, withholding any kind of promotional budget. By late 1975, Aerosmith were graduating to the bigger halls by virtue of word-of-mouth advertising. They'd played under Sabbath, ZZ Top and a host of others, and had won over much of that audience, enabling them to headline their own gigs. Using that as leverage, Steve Leber went back to Columbia one last time. 'There was an instance when if I didn't literally get down on my knees and beg Columbia to release one more single, "Dream On" . . . It sold the first 100,000 albums. Whatever success we got I attribute to our constant level of touring. Not until we'd gotten a gold record did Columbia get behind us.'

'Dream On' was re-released in April of 1975, when it became Aerosmith's first million-seller, racing to number six on the *Billboard* survey. With that, their reputation was secured and they had delivered an all-American classic. Those who had never heard of Aerosmith were now desperate to catch up with what they'd missed, while the press were delighted to descend on an American band that could finally beat the British at their own game. 1976 would be Aerosmith's year. It would also be the beginning of the end.

5

NOBODY'S FAULT?

Even before *Toys In The Attic* was released, there were worrying signs that the band was starting to come part at the seams. In his review of the album, Gordon Fletcher had commented in *Rolling Stone* on the increasing sloppiness that had ruined many of their recent live performances, and it was true to say Aerosmith were becoming ever more erratic as they buckled beneath the strain of their workload, playing here, there and everywhere as they endeavoured to raise their profile. When *Toys* was a hit, they moved into overdrive to capitalise on this newly found success, not wanting to let it slip away, having worked so long and hard for it. And the more they worked, the harder they played, the more stimulants they needed, the more wasted they got. For a while, that had its charm and, given that many audiences were as out of it as the band were, few really noticed anyway. At many shows, nobody knew who they were, where they were or who the band were. That went double for the group.

Aerosmith were widely viewed as an overnight success when 'Dream On' hit the top, but of course that was nonsense. They'd put five years of hard labour into the band and were only now reaping the rewards. What did happen overnight was a massive change in the respect and attention they received from their fellow countrymen. A band that could scarcely get arrested in March 1975, they were feted as heroes by the end of the year. Even Steven Tyler was taken back by this sudden turnaround, noting, 'I always knew I was a musician,

I just never thought it would happen like this. Growin' by leaps and bounds.' The realisation of all their ambitions had much that was positive to commend it. Joey Kramer was especially pleased for it helped him rebuild his own family ties. 'When I quit school to join the band, my dad cut me off. We didn't speak for two, maybe three years. Then one day, when we'd started to sell some records, I bought him a Cadillac. I really couldn't afford it but I bought it anyway, drove it all the way from Boston to Yonkers. I'll never forget the look on my old man's face when I pulled it up the driveway. He could understand the Cadillac. I was OK, I'd made it.'

If Joey was OK financially, his dad might have been more worried if he'd had any idea of what was going on backstage night after night. If all manner of sensual pleasures had been on tap when they were a support act, becoming the headliners provided the keys to their very own toy cupboard. Bored with the routine of touring, Steven and Joey got arrested in Nebraska for setting off fireworks in their hotel room, and Steven narrowly escaped a further period of incarceration when he used the dreaded F-word on-stage in Memphis.

These relatively harmless pranks were symptoms of a creeping malaise that was to strike the band down in the course of the next two years. The writing was on the wall in 1975 though. With the money suddenly pouring in, it started to flow out just as quickly. Following Led Zeppelin's example, they took charge of a private plane to fly them to gigs at enormous cost. The madness continued when, playing a show at Canada's National Exhibition Centre in front of 25,000 fans, the band drove – *drove* – the fifty yards from the dressing-room to the stage in two huge stretch limos! No one in the camp seemed to have any grasp on reality. There were good reasons for that, as Tyler confessed, 'It got to the point where I'd drink an eight-ounce glass of Jack Daniels and fill up my nose with cocaine before I went on-stage, and I'd be flying, man. I once had three Porsches and I sold 'em all so I could snort the whole of Peru. I was paying $1,000 a gram for heroin and doing about three to five grams a week. I'd have traded my nuts in for a good ounce of heroin then.'

Tyler wasn't alone in being consumed by the madness, for all five members of the band, along with the people that surrounded them, were going the same way. No one could warn them of the consequences, because they were all along on the ride. As Kramer said later, 'Nobody could tell us anything anyway. We were at the top, we were the best. If you'd tried to set us straight, you'd have been dead. No question, you'd have been out.' Tyler admitted to the same lack of respect for anyone else's opinion and the occasional bad review drove him to seek further refuge in a bottle. The only real criticism that raised its head throughout 1975 was the Stones rip-off accusations, a short-sighted comparison, based purely on their looks and on-stage behaviour, for musically Aerosmith were a far more sophisticated musical mix. Tyler was predictably livid at such claims, sniping back, 'Anybody who says I'm a Jagger rip-off because I look like him has no intelligence. Joe Perry looks like Keith Richards a little. What are we supposed to do? Get plastic surgery?' Joe Perry was equally frustrated and claimed, 'I know all that hasn't got anything to do with our success. In the States the Stones audience averages twenty-five years of age whereas ours evens out at about seventeen.' Those myths cleared up, each would stomp off to the dressing-room for a little further recreation.

This backstage Babylon was a theme repeated by many bands across America at the time but, since Aerosmith were now among the biggest, they had access to more and more temptations. Since they were driven by the most driven of men, Tyler's compulsions only dragged them closer and closer towards the abyss. The climate was certainly ideal for a band so keen to sample everything that was on offer. Joe Perry admits, 'That was the music business in the 1970s – it wasn't unusual to put three bottles of Jack Daniels on your rider [hospitality] and expect to drink them all, no problem. It just escalates to the point where it's all that you're doing. That was the general atmosphere and we loved it. We really loved it.'

The most surprising thing was that not only did Aerosmith manage to stagger on to the stage in spite of the substances swilling around the collective system, but generally they managed to perform like demons, creating a wholly justified reputation as one of the very best live acts anywhere in the world. The focal point, Tyler, whirled like a dervish, complaining about the lack of quality among the competition. 'I've been going to a lot of concerts lately watching groups who are so fucking outrageous on record that you'd think they'd get out there on-stage and shake ass. But they just stand there. The songs we write aren't the kind that you come out and fucking genuflect. We play kick-ass music!' It was a sentiment picked up by *Sounds*' John Milward who caught a show in Chicago at a time when the British audience was extremely suspicious of US bands in general. 'Aerosmith shoot for kick-ass flash, they drive with a professional energy that the competition lacks . . . the best mid-1960s British rock renovators of American rhythm and blues, twin lead guitars owe more to The Yardbirds than the Allmans.' All in all a resounding endorsement for a band that still had to set foot outside its own country. That would have to wait a little longer for they were determined to get another studio album together as soon as possible while everything was moving in their direction. Columbia, suddenly Aerosmith's biggest fans, and Leber-Krebs were both determined to keep their men working to the most daunting of schedules so that they could continue to reap the financial rewards.

Rocks hit the racks with a vengeance in June 1976, a mere eleven months after *Toys In The Attic* had been released, following a year where Aerosmith had scarcely left the road. With a workload like that, it would have been understandable if it had been a tired and uninspired collection, but the reality was quite the reverse. *Rocks*, well, it rocked, surging with fury and passion, brimming with ideas and invention, characterised by excellent playing by all. In no time at all, it was residing in the top three of the US album charts, effortlessly shifting one million copies and clinching their first platinum record in the process. Looking back while reviewing the Aerosmith CD re-issue programme fifteen years, David Cavanagh wrote in *Q* that *Rocks* was, 'Disgusting, beyond pissed off and highly enjoyable . . . a basically great album. In 1976, they were, very possibly, America's Greatest Rock 'n' Roll Band.' In 1976 no one would have quibbled with that observation. Aerosmith could fill any stadium they chose in the US such was their popularity. On the evidence of *Rocks*, it was a popularity they richly deserved, for it maintained the high standards of *Toys In The Attic*, despite the gruelling schedule that accompanied its making – it has been suggested that so great were the pressures, during the making of *Rocks* Perry succumbed to the seductive charms of heroin, starting a long and expensive addiction.

Be that as it may, the album didn't suffer. Indeed, so prolific were they that *Rocks* was the first album that didn't feature a cover version. Their self-penned material was so good that the album didn't suffer in consequence, but was lifted by the unified nature of the songs. In the course of his *Sounds* review, Geoff Barton noted that 'this LP has the grimiest, raunchiest feel I've come across for some time', something that was dredged from the frazzled psyche of its creators. Working with Jack Douglas again, they worked mainly at the Record Plant, although some material was recorded in the more homely atmosphere of the Wherehouse in Waltham, Massachusetts, away from the distractions of the big city. Maybe that's why they sounded so collectively vicious, simply because they had no other outlet for their frustrations. Whatever the cause, few records are as genuinely, as opposed to theatrically, venomous as this one. Barton commented on Aerosmith's straightforward *modus operandi*: 'Aerosmith work on the well-worn principle that maximum output equals maximum excitement, finesse being not so much a lesser priority as a minor consideration,' and it was true that the subtleties of *Toys In The Attic* were absent from *Rocks*, but the album survived by virtue of its intensity.

'Back In The Saddle' was an impressive opener, cloaked in lovely special effects – as obtrusive as Douglas's production got – and an excellent bass part from the oft undervalued Tom Hamilton. A menacing Western tale, it was obviously intended as an allegorical version of the band's life on the road, gunslingers riding into town, causing havoc, stealing the women, drinking the whiskey and getting out again under cover of night. If that sounded a romantic way of life, the music belied that, suggesting a band on the run, trapped on a treadmill with no chance of jumping off. Tyler had lost the control that had been displayed on *Toys In The Attic*, his voice reduced to a screech, yet the emotion generated by a man trying his best was enough to salvage the song.

Particularly when viewed alongside its predecessors, *Rocks* made it apparent that here was a band whose entire life consisted of, and depended upon, the rock 'n' roll bubble. Virtually every song alluded to touring or recording in some way, rarely in a positive fashion. It was an album whose face was contorted with rage, anger, hatred and paranoia. It was the final time that they would be capable of wrestling those emotions into a cohesive structure and as such, it does represent some kind of peak in the first phase of their career. Listening to it now is almost a guilty pleasure, for in hindsight the songs are so much more comprehensible, the demons besetting them explained by the events of the years that followed its release.

Rocks was the sound of a defiant band going under without even realising they were drowning, a window through which you could watch five men having a collective nervous breakdown. Nowhere was that more readily apparent than in the gutsy 'Nobody's Fault', which reeked of desperation, men without a clue where to turn and with nothing in their head except the identity of the next venue they were heading towards. 'Lick And A Promise' offered a slightly more appealing slant on rock stardom; 'Sick As A Dog' was a witty exposition of the morning after, indicating just how much of a roll they were on, taking a Stones' cliché and adapting it until it became identifiably and enjoyably Aerosmith.

'Combination', Joe Perry's first solo composition, reprised the sentiments of dislocation first touched on in 'Round And Round', further pointing out that the dissolute life wasn't the sole preserve of Tyler, but of the whole group. 'Rats In The Cellar', a kind of answer to 'Toys In The Attic', showed just what can go wrong when you do leave reality behind and run away to join the circus. Its mood of inquisitive self-loathing caught beautifully the push and pull of the peculiar career they had embarked on, curious to pursue the use of stimulants to their conclusion, enjoying the adrenalin rush of crowds and drugs alike, yet hating the machinery that surrounded them, despising the industry that was forcing them onwards at the risk of their health and their reputations, and feeling repugnance with themselves for their descent into the slime, as Tyler put it. The band's distaste for the pushers and the hangers-on was tangible, yet so was their love of their frantic, romanticised life. There was some resolution to this turmoil in the overwrought tongue-in-cheek finale, 'Home Tonight', the classic tear-jerking guitar solo augmenting the relieved desperation of the travelling man who would finally make it back home. Those sentiments were also reinforced in 'Last Child', where the refrain of 'home sweet home' was ironically significant.

That was Aerosmith's problem in a nutshell. They hated the drudgery of being in a band, yet could never settle in one place, a few days' rest and recuperation being all they reckoned they needed before setting out for the war, where the cycle would begin again. It was time that Tyler and company started to worry about breaking that connection, as opposed to losing their drug supplying connection, the thought which exercised his mind in 'Rats In The Cellar'.

Their success wasn't going to go away, so things weren't going to quieten down for a while yet. *Rolling Stone* praised, 'A return to the ear-boxing sound that made *Get Your wings* their best. The guitar riffs and Steven Tyler's cat-like voice fairly jump out of the speakers . . . while they can be accused of neither profundity nor originality, Aerosmith's stylised hard-rock image and sound pack a high-energy punch most other heavy metal bands lack.' Geoff Barton concurred with the view in *Sounds*, adding, 'Despite an over-abundance of influences, Aerosmith do manage to retain an individual sound, primarily down to Tyler's breathtaking vocal work. Not for migraine sufferers.' Lauded to the skies, *Rocks* hasn't worn quite as well as *Toys In The Attic*, which was a little more varied and stylish. It has been *Toys* that has survived as the legacy of the early days, but as a snapshot of a moment in their career, *Rocks* is infinitely more vivid, capturing a band actually living through their music. As a consequence, it's much more personal and considerably more scary.

Rocks was as unified and powerful as it got for Aerosmith, a last hurrah as the cracks began to appear. Having already booked a huge tour, they had to cut short the recording time, possibly accounting for the fact that the album lasted a mere thirty-four minutes. Ironically, this very shortage of material was a positive boost for the album. It's fair to say that hard rock records are best kept short and punchy for it's impossible for both listener and artist to sustain the necessary level of pure energy to make it work for more than forty minutes. With the advent of the CD, many artists have tried to offer value for money with albums that reach sixty or seventy minutes in length, but often that has lessened the impact. The very limitations that vinyl put on bands – after more than twenty minutes of music on one side, the vinyl becomes incapable of faithfully replaying all the musical frequencies and nuances – helped create some of the very best albums ever made. By concentrating minds wonderfully and forcing artists to hone the material to the bare minimum, wasteful self-indulgence was often avoided in a way it isn't today.

Even so, thirty-four minutes wasn't a lot to get your teeth in to. Tyler admitted, 'I couldn't even stay for the mixes. We had already cancelled two weeks of dates because of some final mastering. I insist on being there. I know what went down, what we wanted to do. Since having so much to do with the songs, I wanted at least to be able to mix them a little bit but I had to get back out there. I want to know where the edits are going. It shouldn't all be left to the producer but we had no choice this time.' The determination to get back out to their faithful following was crippling the group, yet such was the advanced state of paranoia that was eating away at the Aerosmith camp, they could see no solution. Tyler conceded that the fault was largely theirs, their monumental ambition overriding any other consideration, while they lacked the wit to invent alternative strategies. 'We spent the whole of the 1970s on a treadmill. We'd stay out on the road for a year and a half, and the only time we'd come off was to record. There was no MTV so all you did was tour if you were lucky. We wanted to make it Big Time, so we worked and worked.'

Even so, they were starting to hate the whole rigmarole. A show at the Anaheim Stadium, headlining before 56,000 fans, showed just how far and how fast things were racing downhill. *Sounds'* Justin Pierce reviewed the concert: 'Aerosmith have acted like stars since their inception and their attitude has been crucial in gaining the band a following. Audiences are easily swayed by images and Aerosmith's punk-rock stance has taken them far . . .. The group started 'Dream On' but suddenly Tyler blurted, "Stop it. Yeah, I'm gettin' sick of that fuckin' song".' What appeared to loyal supporters as typical Aerosmith behaviour, put on for show, was actually quite the reverse. The band were genuinely sick of it all and desperately needed time off.

Groups can be pushed to their limits especially when record companies are eager to recoup their heavy investments while the band are riding high. There's no suggestion that as reputable a management team as Leber-Krebs would have had any truck with such dubious methods, but Joe Perry said later, 'We were isolated from our friends, families and anybody who was sane. The people around us fostered that isolation. We were paranoid and we were trapped.' Far more, it was the business itself, along with the band's own weaknesses that had ensnared Aerosmith, for they needed the shows, the drink, the drugs to give their existence any validity. Stardom wasn't now a means to an end – a life playing music – but was an end in itself. The rot had truly set in.

It still had its irresistible compensations though, for as real rock stars they were able to meet their idols. Steven Tyler, not one who was easily impressed by anything, found himself utterly star struck by a meeting with Mick Jagger, which in itself was confirmation that he had arrived. 'I met Mick, spent two days with him. Blew my head. We had a blast, got along real well. Me and Woody are the best of friends and have been for years, but I'd never met Mick before. It blew my head. He was just climbing out of the sauna, standing there in a towel and went "Steven!" just like that. It was beautiful, I was very happy. We talked about you name it. We sat around all night singing songs, makin' up songs. Woody was playing the guitar, just sittin' around, shootin' the shit.'

Sadly for every great moment like that, there were many days when everything seemed to be going wrong. In their drug-addled state, the smallest inconvenience assumed enormous proportions, and Aerosmith became synonymous with brattish backstage behaviour, tearing down dressing-rooms if everything wasn't done to their complete satisfaction. Steven admitted, 'I was doing things just because I could. I'd think nothing of tipping over a table with a long spread on it just because there was turkey roll on the table and I had explicitly said "no turkey roll" before the gig. I would come in after coming off-stage and I'd have twelve ounces of Jack Daniels in me, a gram of coke, sweating profusely, and I'd see a tray with turkey roll on it. I'd just turn the whole thing right over. It felt good.'

Although Tyler and the band were ostensibly under the influence of drugs, that was not the only cause of such ludicrous tantrums. Essentially, they were revelling in the power they now had. After all the years of struggle, suddenly everyone wanted to know them, everyone wanted to tell them how great they were, everyone wanted to please. Simultaneously delighted with their privileges and disgusted by the obsequious manner of those hangers on, the band were happy to test the limits of everyone's endurance, knowing that they were in total control – if the promoter didn't like it, they wouldn't play. Given that every other facet of their career – where to play, when to play, when to record – was out of their hands, given that their personal lives were uncontrollable thanks to the drugs and drink, it was little wonder that they chose to take out their frustrations in such a childish, but relatively innocuous way.

Digging further, it's clear that personality clashes within the group were threatening to wreck everything. Joe Perry explained, 'I saw this documentary about gorillas. When two of them get together, they'll throw shit but they won't throw it at each other. They'll just make a lot of noise. That's what Steven and I would do. We'd get in the dressing-room and tear it apart but we never laid a hand on each other. But there was so much anger. If we were in a different space, we'd have killed each other.' The differences in personality between the perfectionist Tyler and the relaxed Perry, which had caused musical sparks to fly, was now having its inevitable effect on their personal lives, exacerbated by the fraught circumstances in which they lived. *Rocks* had shown one of the reasons for the problem when there had been no room for any cover versions. Where on *Aerosmith* Tyler had been the pre-eminent writer, Perry was now challenging that position, writing more and more of the music. This had financial implications for it was reducing Tyler's share of the publishing royalties, but it was the question of recognition that mattered most.

The majority of hard rock bands have to maintain a delicate balance between their two prime movers and, very often, prima donnas, the lead singer and the lead guitarist. It's the chemistry that exists between them which can make a band work – Plant and Page, Jagger and Richards, Gillan and Blackmore, Axl and Slash. Aerosmith had started out as Steven Tyler's group, but more and more fans and critics were now citing Joe Perry as his equal, if not superior in the band's hierarchy. Without Perry's contribution, there would have been no 'Walk This Way' or 'Back In The Saddle', for instance. Perry was happy to receive his deserved share of the glory, but equally naturally Tyler was upset, and there was a virulent strain of jealousy existing between them which only served to increase the tension in the camp. At times they could work together and could enjoy the childish pranks that enlivened touring, such as experimenting with gunpowder – a shattered guitar was the result of that practical joke. When things weren't going so smoothly, all hell could break loose, Steven remembering, 'We used to fight on-stage. Joe could torment me to death by not giving me a line of dope. I'd go over and push him while he was playing and he'd hit me with the guitar. He stuck the end of a guitar string through my lower lip once so I spat blood all over him.'

Even amid all this chaos, the two could still unite in the attempt to take Aerosmith on to the next level of popularity. With the US conquered they wanted to cast their net further, looking over to Europe, their first visit coming in the autumn of 1976. The tour turned into a nightmare, financially – they insisted on bringing their private plane to fly between British gigs at a phenomenal cost which far outstripped the box office take – and logistically. The shows weren't a huge success either, with British audiences particularly mistrustful of a group who were muscling in on Zeppelin's territory. *Sounds*' Barbara Charone was similarly chauvinistic when she noted that, at Hammersmith Odeon, 'When Tyler and Perry came together to sing, visually they look like miniature Jagger and Richards dolls. If they sang out of tune they'd be perfect . . . Tyler knows all the tricks from the Jack Daniels manly rock star swig to the ability to rouse an audience . . . a weird assortment of Led Zeppelin riffs and mysticism, Status Quo simplicity and Alice Cooper aggression, Aerosmith are the first full-bodied classic British rock 'n' roll band of the 1970s. And they're American. Star quality – ten. Presentation – ten. Content – four.'

Despite the trials and tribulations of this first visit, Aerosmith returned the following year in what marked a watershed for the group. They had yet to produce a follow-up to *Rocks* twelve months after its release and the demands that Columbia were putting on them to fulfil their contract were taking their toll, just as Leber-Krebs were insisting that they should try to crack the lucrative European market wide open. The Reading Festival seemed a good way of playing to the maximum number of Brits in the shortest time, so they lined up a slot there on the second day, interrupting studio work to fly over. So unknown were they, they were second on the bill to Graham Parker

And The Rumour, with John Miles and Thin Lizzy sharing the day. Tyler tried to rationalise this apparent demotion by arguing that it was what they'd wanted from the outset. 'It gives you an edge, gives you something to prove, it'll bring the fun back like the old days when we used to open for Mott the Hoople. It's just a different kick, just go out and kick ass and not give a shit about what we're doing.'

The set was well received, but there was no sudden seismic growth in their popularity ratings. Much of the comment inevitably surrounded Tyler's Jaggerisisms and his extravagant use of the microphone stand, draping it with scarves, hurling it around like a spear. 'Why do I drag the microphone stand around? 'Cos if it's not there when I go for it, I got nothin' to sing into. I get so disorientated on-stage sometimes I go to grab it and forget where I left it. It's my toy, it's my thing, that's why I put scarves on it – myself and Francine Larnis do the costumes. I need things that'll give, I like the open front to a certain extent, I like having a tail, I like things that flow, so the scarves form part of that. But the stand is my friend. It gets cold sometimes. I have to take good care of Mike.'

The stand was yet another crutch for the crumbling Tyler to rest on, but the scarves had a dual purpose as he later confessed. 'I snorted and drank but my other thing was barbiturates, Tuinals, Seconals, heavy narcotic pills. My metabolism is such that when I take a Tuinal, I wanna clear the room, go rehearse. I'm the complete opposite of most people. Get fucked up the night before and wake up feeling great. That's why I'm an addict. You know that little scarf I used to wear round my neck on stage? When we came to England in 1977, that thing was filled with Tuinals. It was like a condom, it had a little hole at the top, I would hold on to 'em while we were playing. Feel 'em, count 'em.'

Along with the Reading Festival, they played a few mainland European shows too. Heading into Germany, Tyler was arrested and briefly held for possession of cannabis, Perry explaining the cowboy analogy of 'Back In The Saddle' by remarking, 'We thought we were outlaws because we were always carrying drugs.' It marked the end of Aerosmith's flirtation with Europe because as Tyler recounted, 'After that, we never left the States 'cos we were too scared to go through customs.'

America still offered many compensations though. So important were Aerosmith to Columbia that the band were invited to corporate functions, a pretty risky move given the band's wayward reputation. Perry remembers, 'They wanted us at a CBS convention in 1977 to present the reps with platinum records. Everyone was at The Century City Hotel but we said, "We stay at The Beverly Hills Hotel, or we don't come." We were there with the liquor tab of $5,000 because all the bands came over to party with us. The waiters were in a bucket brigade, we went on the phone to room service every twelve minutes. All we had to say was what we wanted and that was it. The thinking was "Who knows how long this is going to last? In the meantime, have fun".'

It's astonishing to think that in 1977 with millions of records sold, Aerosmith might still feel that the whole thing could evaporate tomorrow and that they should enjoy the party while it lasted. What is yet more amazing is that no one ever took them in hand and pointed out to them that, if they took their songwriting and recording seriously, they would have a licence to print money for ever more. Instead, they chose to burn the dollars that their hard work was earning. Steven Tyler knew what was happening to him: 'I lose four pounds a night on tour so I'm kinda zzzz after the show. It's nuts. We don't usually get much time to rehearse. We start the tour out in one or two small houses, which of course won't happen any more, and then do a lot of soundchecks. Come in at five-thirty and rehearse for an hour until they open the doors on us. But there's never time to do anything. We work so hard that you get road warp. You lose contact when you go from airplane to hotel room from limo to hall to hotel, and that's it . . . two more years like this and I'll be in a silly farm.' They all chose to ignore the warning signs. How dumb could they get?

6

DUMB AND DUMBER

On the release of the ultra-impressive *Rocks*, Joe Perry remarked, 'It's getting better with everyone, the songs are more unified and the whole band's coming up with worthwhile ideas. I'm looking forward to the next one because I know it'll be better again. We're managing to get into a groove in the studio now and we're trying to keep it that way.' The next album didn't surface until January 1978, eighteen months later, by which time Aerosmith were a completely different unit to the one that previously had been so focused.

It was in June of 1977 that they upped sticks to a disused monastery, The Cenacle in Armon, New York state, in order to put the new *magnum opus* together. It proved to be a disastrous decision. *Draw The Line*, as the album became known, cost Aerosmith a million bucks to record, taking the thick end of six months to compile. Just a cursory look at the sleevenotes made it very apparent that something was seriously wrong – the Tyler/Perry songwriting partnership that had been so fruitful and had been such an integral part of their success could produce a mere three tracks. Meanwhile the other four members of the group had written two songs without looking for any contribution from Joe. Given the way the record was put together that was no surprise, for the increasingly estranged Perry could rarely bear even to be in the same room as Tyler for any length of time. Consequently, he is more notable for his absence than for any great contribution to *Draw The Line*. The album therefore lacked his considerable qualities as an aggressive but melodic axe murderer.

Indeed *Rolling Stone* was forced to report, 'For a riff-based band to come up with only one outstanding guitar hook on an entire LP is beyond belief.'

Reports from the album sessions suggest that once Perry had put down his guitar parts, he locked himself away in a wholly separate wing of the monastery, sat slumped in a chair, whiling away the hours by shooting at targets with a handgun. Listening to the album, it sounds as if while he was away, his contributions were either buried or wiped. Given Tyler's antipathy towards him at this stage, exacerbated by the inclusion of 'Bright Light Fright' with Perry as lead vocalist and over which Tyler was vociferous in his complaints, that is extremely likely. Perry commented later, '*Draw the Line* marks the point where we got more interested in the deal than the music, the songs didn't matter any longer. Before I left home to make that record, I spent a week at home making a demo of six songs that I put on cassette. By the time I got to the studio I couldn't find it. Couldn't remember the songs either. That's where my head was. Luckily, my ex-wife found it in the cookie jar.' Tyler's contemporary comment on it all was an arch 'Bad chemistry, man. We'd been on the road for too long, spent a lot of our money and a couple of the guys got married. Joe was paying more attention to his wife than to his music.' Although later he confessed, 'We allowed ourselves to be pushed into a corner and we just went crazy,' his remark about the attention Perry paid his wife and child were pertinent to the breakdown in their relations. Tyler himself had no children and had generally treated the string of women that adorned his arm as mere accessories. For him, the band had always been more important than any woman could ever be. In addition, he knew that his musical alliance with Perry was fundamental to the band's future, even though he would never have said as much. Perry was his best friend, his artistic collaborator, his drink and drugs partner. They might fight, but as long as Tyler had Joe and any drug of his choice, there was fun to be had. Now that partnership was being threatened by outside influences, and Tyler reacted jealously, lashing out at this apparent betrayal. In his state of incipient paranoia, he felt that even his closest colleagues had turned against him and the bonds between them quickly dissolved, finally turning their relationship into one of pure hatred.

In fairness to Tyler, Perry was never the easiest man to know, always keeping his cards close to his chest. Tyler was a compulsive talker, effusive, eager to please by revealing anything and everything about himself, but Perry was remote, an observer of those around him. In the early days of Aerosmith, that was important, for both had to dedicate themselves to their music and their work. Perry liked to absorb himself completely in his current obsession, and as long as that was Aerosmith, he and Tyler had no problems. Once the band had hit the big time, once Joe was finding success as much a pain as a pleasure, his interest moved elsewhere, and understandably he focused more attention on his family as both an escape and an obligation. Tyler couldn't cope with that shift of emphasis, for he was always looking towards the next record, turning platinum into double-platinum, selling twice as many concert tickets. As things between them deteriorated, like an old married couple Perry knew exactly how to upset Tyler the most, by withdrawing further and further from him. As he sat alone in his room in the monastery, with each shot that he fired, he must have taken solace from the fact that each bullet drove Tyler just a little more crazy.

So what of *Draw The Line*? The first shock came with the sleeve. It dispensed with their logo and carried no name, just a striking Al Hirschfeld caricature of the group. It acted as a bold statement that Aerosmith had arrived, that they were wholly secure, and that their records could sell on the back of a cartoon sketch. Such arrogance had long been a part of their act, but it had now deteriorated into a state of smug over-confidence, built on the belief that whatever atonal rubbish they released, people would buy it. It was true that people flocked to the stores to buy *Draw The Line*, and it secured platinum status with the greatest of ease, but this time it peaked at number eleven, a disappointment as *Rocks* had reached number three. At the time, Tyler ascribed this to the fact, 'We weren't on the road when it came out and that was a big mistake.' In truth, people didn't buy it because it was a lousy record, though Columbia did them few favours either. Choosing the title track as the lead-off single in December 1977 must rank among the greatest tactical errors in the history of music marketing. It was an unbelievable selection. Cacaphonic crap, it was claustrophobic, chaotic, unmelodic, dense

America's greatest rock 'n' roll band fresh from the attic. Clockwise from top –
Hamilton, Whitford, Perry, Tyler, Kramer, 1975.

Above: Aerosmith check
their deodorant – Tyler,
Hamilton, Perry, Whitford,
Kramer, 1976.

Left: 'I'll have a very large
black coffee and keep your
hands off that stash!' Tyler's
going up in 1976.

Washington's RFK Stadium, 1979. 180,000 reach the parts that other substances cannot reach.

Steven Tyler flirts with lung cancer.

Above: Aerosmith get a grip – Tyler, Whitford, Hamilton, Kramer, Perry, 1992.

Below: Tyler has a quiet word in Perry's ear.

Above: Steven and Perry fly the flag.

THIS SIGN HELPS
PROTECT LIFE
HELP US PROTECT
THIS SIGN
COLUMBIA CO. HGY. DEPT.

Left: Steven's got a gun, 1995.

The Toxic Twins get back in the saddle.

Steven Tyler prepares to eat the rich.

and totally incomprehensible. With that as the taster for the album, people figured that the other songs would be even worse and left *Draw The Line* in the shops.

Sadly, that title track *was* one of the best things on the album, along with Joe Perry's singing début 'Bright Light Fright' and the experimental progressive-rock-tinged 'Kings And Queens'. The former was yet another trawl through the 'living out of a suitcase' lifestyle of the rock star, though at least this time it was coherently structured, despite its frenetic pace. Sketchily detailing his vampiric existence – going to bed as the sun comes up and never seeing the daylight – it was as lyrically competent as anything Tyler could come up with by now. Unfortunately though, it was merely raking over old ground for the audience had heard everything there was to hear about their private lives on the previous albums. There is a very definite limit to how many times you can make a valid statement about life on the road being tough, and Aerosmith had gone way beyond it. The ordinary fans who bought their albums and had elevated the band to their exalted position might be working in a garage, a factory, an office or in the local store in Columbus, Ohio, scraping together just enough cash to buy the new record and the concert ticket. They knew how hard life could really be. A privileged rock band with money coming out of their ears didn't. Tales of limos, private planes, drink and girls hurling themselves at you had no resonance for the fans any longer – at first these tales were exotic and compelling, but now they were just tedious. Aerosmith simply weren't producing anything that the fans could relate to any longer.

On 'Bright Light Fright', Perry bemoaned that he was out of 'zoom', a statement that was true of the whole group, for inspiration was terribly thin on the ground. The aforementioned 'Kings And Queens' was the only real departure and on such a desperately inconsequential record as this, it was seized on with relish. Put together in the studio by Tyler, Hamilton, Whitford, Kramer and producer Jack Douglas, there was an intriguing musicality to it, Tyler adding piano and Douglas mandolin. Tyler said, 'We've recorded some heady things. "Kings And Queens" was about conflicts, reality and fantasy, commerce and art. We're not all "Walk This Way".' But in truth, so densely was it recorded, it was hard to pick out the lyrics,

Rolling Stone's Billy Altman noting, 'Rarely have Tyler's lyrics been mixed so low and the few times the lyrics are discernible, they disappoint.'

It was becoming an aggravating, finally fatal, trait of Tyler's that he was becoming increasingly late with his lyrics, often making them up virtually on the spot, which explained why Douglas was forced to mask them in among the instrumentation. In addition, the concentrated rage of *Rocks* had been dulled to be replaced by the words of a man who could only throw disjointed, incoherent tantrums.

'I Wanna Know Why' was perhaps the clearest song, yet it was dull hard rock with no focus, cloaked in paranoia. 'Critical Mass', possibly a snipe at the press, was a sloppy blues with a truly dreadful vocal, Tyler cracking palpably and painfully under the strain. 'Get It Up' spelled out the problems, manager Krebs remarking, 'The essence of Aerosmith's lyrics is a positive macho sexuality. Definitely anti-feminist. "Draw The Line" wasn't like that. The song "Get It Up" really says "can't get it up". Kids who are stoned and having sex don't want to hear that.' The song was flaccid and impotent Rolling-Stones-by-numbers, comprehensively lacking in wit and invention, full of abysmal puns, with the guitar part seemingly deliberately blocked out. If you can criticise Tyler for being childish in apparently delighting in deleting Perry's work, you must also ask what was Perry doing by allowing this to happen. Everything around Aerosmith was a shambles, rotting, miserable and sordid.

Perry was forced to confess later, 'The expensive thing isn't the drug, even the amount we were doing. It's the decisions you make or don't make while you're fucked up. You can tell exactly what happened to us by listening to the records. From inside, I didn't think anything was wrong, but from outside you could see everything. You can hear the music get cloudy. On *Draw The Line*, the focus is gone.' Aerosmith's days were numbered, but none of them were in a fit state to see it, so they just limped on and on. If the proud band that had made *Toys In The Attic* had realised that one day that they would make something as toe-curlingly atrocious as 'The Hand That Feeds', they'd have disbanded there and then, but by now there was no sense of quality control and anything would do. 'Sight For Eyes', a collaboration with ex-New York Doll, David Johansen, was astoundingly dull, memorable only because Tyler was very soon to marry Johansen's ex-wife Cyrinda Fox, who he was busily ensnaring as the song was being written. The album closed, not a moment too soon, with an insipid and completely pointless retread of 'Milk Cow Blues', bringing down the curtain on Aerosmith's most dispiriting hour. The search for any redeeming feature was a long and fruitless one. With every previous album they'd made, you could play it and later that day you'd find yourself singing 'Dream On', 'Same Old Song And Dance', 'Toys In The Attic', 'Walk This Way', 'Sweet Emotion', 'Back In The Saddle', 'Sick As A Dog', or 'Home Tonight'. But there wasn't one song that stayed in the mind even after a dozen plays of *Draw The Line*. With hindsight, *Q* termed the album 'muddily produced, heads down, backs to the wall'; *Vox* complained of 'the same tired old blues licks trundled out again.'

Oddly, at the time of its release, the British press received the record warmly, though the public continued to ignore Aerosmith – the British view was that we already had our own Led Zeppelin thanks very much, so we didn't need another one, especially one from the US. However Geoff Barton gave the record a rave reception, telling *Sounds*' readers, 'You've only got to spin *Draw The Line* through once to come to the inescapable conclusion that Aerosmith are a bloody fine rock 'n' roll band and that this album is a seething testimony to the fact . . . it thrashes along in the same breathless hell-for-leather fashion as *Rocks*, numbers colliding with each other with cataclysmic results, Steven Tyler in frighteningly frenzied mood screaming wildly as his voice threatens to be swamped by scintillating Joe Perry guitar work . . . does a lot to restore Aerosmith's credibility.'

And such credibility was quickly undermined by a crass CBS campaign that suggested that English rock fans were ignoring Aerosmith out of anti-American prejudice, adding that they could draw the line at the established British names, but in doing so 'you'll be ignoring some of the best American hard rock you're ever likely to hear.' This may have been fair comment, but to tell your potential converts that they were stupid and chauvinistic wasn't the most intelligent of campaign strategies.

If *Billboard* termed Aerosmith a 'legitimate supergroup', back home the majority of critics were scathing in their condemnation. Inevitably, *Rolling Stone* was harsh on this dismal mish-mash, Billy Altman writing that it was 'a truly horrendous record, chaotic to the point of malfunction and with an almost impenetrably dense sound adding to the confusion.' Curiously though, he found some light among the despair, adding, 'These guys are not evil conmen selling stolen goods. If they were, this record would be a lot better than it is since anyone can repeat a formula. Aerosmith sounds like a band starting out, like amateurs. You may think me perverse but that gives me hope.' Amateurish they were without doubt, but rather than a band setting out in the world, *Draw The Line* sounded like a group at the end of the line, world-weary musicians who couldn't care less any more as long as the money kept flowing in. Worse than the poor songwriting and playing that it showcased, it illustrated a band without a soul. Tyler had to admit to that later on, saying, 'I wrote a lot of great songs on a shot of blow and a line of heroin, but it's a two-edged sword. It frees you up but then it steals your spirit, and spirituality is what music is all about. I was scared to death to clean up, I couldn't have fun without it. I started stealing and stuff. Its like an initiation, you take drugs to be with the devil and be creative, and it works for a while, but then he goes "Ha! Ha! Now I'm going to steal your soul," and he does. I can't pretend we didn't have a good time doing that, it just nearly killed us in the end. To survive the 1970s was a miracle.'

Ironically, Leber-Krebs were starting to suggest at this stage that the groundwork had been done and the band could ease off a little, Krebs arguing in typically macho style that 'the thing that separates the men from the boys is that they stick with it; we reached the top in 1977 so we switched from a running game to a passing game.' It was too late by now, the damage had been done to the band and they had produced the worst record of their career, so the passing-game idea was already redundant. To attempt at winning the group world-wide exposure, even though Aerosmith couldn't travel outside the US because of their drug habits, other forms of promotion had to be uncovered. Robert Stigwood was producing a movie based on The Beatles' *Sergeant Pepper's Lonely Hearts Club Band*, starring Peter

Frampton and The Bee Gees. True to form, Aerosmith were signed up as the film's baddies, playing The Future Villain Band. Ultimately, the group were seen off in a fight between Tyler and Frampton, though such was Tyler's ego he refused to be beaten by a punch, insisting that instead he lose his balance and fall to his fate.

The film was an unmitigated disaster, a turkey of the first order, destroying plans for Aerosmith to star in their own feature film based on The Future Villain Band. Even so, Tyler's boast that 'I think Aerosmith came off best in that movie' was accurate, if nothing to write home about. Recording The Beatles' 'Come Together' in August 1978 for the film soundtrack, the band briefly realised once more just why they'd started a band in the first place, producing a fresh and vibrant take on Lennon's 1969 classic. Perry sensibly noted, 'You can't change Beatles' songs, they were always perfect, but just to play it was a great charge for us. We did "Come Together" with George Martin and he told us just to play it like the record 'cos it's bound to be different enough just because it's five different musicians playing there.' The single reached number twenty-eight in the US in September 1978, their first hit since 'Last Child' in August 1976. Sadly though, the film failed to produce the boost to their profile around the globe that Leber-Krebs had envisioned, *Sgt. Pepper's Lonely Hearts Club Band* consigned to the ranks of those movies best forgotten, even in that twilight world of satellite TV re-runs.

Aerosmith stayed out on the road in the US, trying to claw back the popularity lost with *Draw The Line*. They had no trouble attracting crowds, for they could still put on a good show when the spirit moved them. Sadly, it was starting to move them less and less frequently. Joe Perry remembered, 'Around then, we'd play songs twice because we forgot we'd already played them. We were in the trenches, and to go on-stage dope-sick and aching meant we were men. But I guess our shows can't have sucked because people came back.' Even the loyalty of their long-suffering supporters was treated with the utmost contempt, Perry sadly recalling, 'We drank to keep the vibe; if we feel good maybe the audience will. But then after a while, we didn't care if anyone else felt good. If you listen to our records, it definitely gets diluted. We started to lose sight of it, we started to see how screwed up we could get before we walked on-stage just to see if we could get away with it. We were literally on our knees trying to find blow.' Tyler concurs, adding, 'Jerry Garcia said we were the druggiest bunch of guys The Grateful Dead had ever seen. They were worried about us, so that gives you some idea!'

Drugs were an attractive escape route as all five could see the carefully constructed Aerosmith edifice crashing down around them. Everything around them only served to further encourage a paranoid siege mentality. In 1978, Perry was hit by stray bullet from a handgun on-stage in Philadelphia. On their return to the city of brotherly love a few months later, he was grazed by a fragment of a beer bottle that had been hurled towards the stage and which had rebounded off Tyler's mike stand. Briefly, the group performed behind a wire mesh for their own protection as audiences fuelled by a vicious cocktail of drink and drugs threatened to run riot at every show – the *What It Takes* video succinctly reprises those times. Aerosmith were lucky to avoid the fate that befell The Who a year later when eleven fans were killed in a stampede for seats in Cincinnati. The impact that kind of disaster might have had on the delicate mental health of the band is incalculable. Despite their irresponsible attitude to their shows, there was a very real bond between group and audience, and a disaster on such a scale would have been devastating. In Wayne, Indiana, for example, twenty-eight kids were arrested at a gig for possession of cannabis. Tyler had them all bailed out and then got the tour accountant to turn up at the court hearings and pay the fines from the band's account at a cost of $4,200. It was such acts of generosity that helped them maintain the fragile goodwill of the public to such an extent that, despite the dip in their commercial fortunes, in the spring of 1978, Aerosmith were able to headline the California Jam festival, playing in front of 350,000 people.

The problem wasn't a purely chemical one, though, for Aerosmith were collectively suffering from the vertigo that afflicts many bands that manage to fly higher than they ever dreamt possible. Joey Kramer hinted at both that and at the creative atrophy that sets in, having to repeat former glories night after night in different cities, simply to keep the cash rolling in – and so expensive were their lifestyles, they needed every cent they could get. 'Playing the same things can get boring a lot of the time. I used to be in a soul band and

I'm really into playing that kind of stuff. But we're one of the biggest rock 'n' roll bands in the world. I've just begun to think about that lately. I don't think we'll ever get bigger. The next step would be to become the Stones or The Who and I don't think there's room to be a rock 'n' roll legend anymore. So I keep playing. And I figure I'm lucky.'

Having achieved success, the trick was to hold on to it, particularly when you've placed a ceiling on your ambitions as Kramer had. Of course, Tyler would have none of that, imagining that Aerosmith could become the biggest thing ever. Yet Kramer was right, for the times were changing, there was a musical changing of the guard taking place at the close of the 1970s. Punk rock and the new wave took charge for a brief period and in truth, it was about time. Hard rock as a genre was increasingly bloated and overblown, its stars ever more remote and isolated. Although Aerosmith had the right attitude – they were white punks on dope after all – everything they stood for had had its day. Throwing away thousands of dollars on recording and on lavish stage-sets, cultivating ruinously expensive cocaine habits, playing on tiny stages to people who were so far away they couldn't see you even with the aid of the most powerful binoculars known to man, these were things that had to go. Go they did, the legend of rock 'n' roll going with them, although that was as much to do with a changing popular culture as anything else. Music was no longer the only, or even the central issue in young people's lives, but merely one of many leisure choices. No band would ever repeat the sheer ubiquity of The Beatles, for no band could ever matter that much again.

So that question once more. Where do you go when you've reached the top? And what do you do once you've worked out the inescapably logical answer?

7

DEAD IN THE WATER

Hopelessly out of it they might have been, but no one in Aerosmith was daft enough to believe that *Draw The Line* represented anything other than a severe lapse in form. The 'passing game' that Leber-Krebs wanted to initiate was now not so much a tactical ploy as an absolute necessity, for the band were literally on their knees. It seemed that the only thing that might save Aerosmith would be a complete break to recharge the batteries, hoping that absence from one another might make the heart grow a little fonder. They got a fortnight.

The Draw The Line tour was perfunctory, if still relatively successful. They were testing their hard-core audience to the limit, though, their extra-curricular antics having more and more impact on the shows. Brad Whitford explained, 'The problem was we just weren't good at drinking. Some bands can get blasted and go on and play a brilliant show but we'd fall over, mess stuff up and generally make fools of ourselves. There's only so long you can do that before the cracks start to appear.' Tyler later recalled, 'Falling down on stage and not being able to get up because I'd had too much whiskey. The kids were chanting "Tyler, Tyler" and I couldn't even get up. It was so embarrassing, I felt so dumb. Now I can only hope that the kids learnt from me. If they can be made aware of what can happen, if they only knew what someone lying dead on the floor from shooting up looks like – I don't think you'd have to worry. I'm thankful that it all happened to me on-stage and not while I was driving a car.' In fact, Tyler did have similar blackouts at the wheel. Driving his jeep, he had a seizure, hit the accelerator, rammed a tree and passed out with a loaded shotgun at his side. Not to be outdone, Perry was cleared for take-off in his private plane while flying in a very different sense, and had to be pulled off the tarmac by police.

Sensibly, with the Draw The Line tour finished, Columbia amounted a holding operation to give the group time off, time to get fit, and to prepare a new killer album. In January of 1979 they released *Live Bootleg*, a bone-crunching collection of pile-driving performances that did a great deal to restore their ailing reputation with its carefully selected material. A platinum seller, it reached number thirteen on the *Billboard* charts, perfectly respectable for a live record. Packaged shoddily to capture the genuine bootleg feel, *Sounds'* Geoff Barton was impressed, terming it, 'No ordinary example of the double live album genre. Calling the disc a bootleg was a stroke of genius . . . musically it's Aerosmith in the raw; very brash, very noisy, ill-refined and often quite badly played, but at all times an incredible amount of live energy scorches through. One hell of a live album deserving of your immediate attention. In the US, the prevailing view wasn't quite so complimentary, as the Aerosmith backlash was already in full swing. *Rolling Stone* noted that by now Aerosmith were so divorced from their roots that they were solely about attitude rather than music. 'The title isn't a conceit, the album sounds like it was recorded in a shoe box using two tin cans and a couple of yards of telephone wire . . . it doesn't make any difference if Aerosmith's music is any good or not. If Steven Tyler's cheeks could talk would they say "We suck" or merely blow the fans a kiss?'

Proving conclusively that Aerosmith did have it in them to be a great band, *Live Bootleg* was meant as a punctuation mark, but it could so easily have been their requiem. The really hard reconstruction work had to start immediately, addressing the dismal failings of the previous studio record. The first move was to replace Jack Douglas in the producer's chair with Gary Lyons, who had worked with Foreigner and The Grateful Dead. The idea was clearly to sharpen things up in the studio, to bring in a fresh face with new ideas to try to jolt the band out of their indolent apathy. Prior to starting work, the band were granted a short break, Tyler illustrating the shocking state of mind he was in. 'It was cool to have a $750 Porsche watch. I went through nine of them. When I got pissed off, I'd wing it across the room. I was so far out, I felt I had to trash something quickly. After I got home from the road, I would wake up in the morning and dial 0 for room service. That was the lunacy I was basing my life on, I couldn't get out of it.'

In truth, at that stage, no break would have been long enough to repair the cracks for, short of checking into five different rehab centres and severing all existing ties with the music industry until they were restored to the rudest health, Aerosmith was beyond redemption. Tom Hamilton magnanimously accepted his share of the blame, pointing out, 'I don't think Steve and Joe should carry the entire rap for what happened in those days. We all enjoyed the twenty-four-hour-a-day-seven-days-a-week partying at first, but it turned into a nightmare.' The scars were mental as much as physical. They continued to drink and take drugs to blot out the God-awful mess they were making of the band and, of course, the more they drank, the worse the band got, so they drank more to blot that out. It seemed inevitable that Aerosmith would have to call it quits.

Maybe that's what they wanted deep down, an excuse to get off the chain gang, a chance to get back to normal lives. They'd answered the questions asked at the end of the last chapter – the only way was down, for to maintain their position at the pinnacle required harder work and greater self-discipline than they were ready to employ. If you were going to go down, you could go down fighting, or you could go out with a whimper. As a group, they were paralysed with indecision as to which route to take.

Joe Perry was the only member of the tribe who seemed keen to give the band one last shot. Possibly he felt guilt at his own feeble input to *Draw The Line*, perhaps he had been energised by the thought of playing music again and sweeping away all the trappings of rock stardom. Maybe he wanted to get back to his rock 'n' roll roots. When the band reconvened in May 1979 to make their sixth, vitally important, studio album, Perry was the one who tried to run the show, turning up with a wealth of material and song ideas. Unfortunately, Tyler interpreted this encouraging move as an attempt to usurp his authority in the band and began to retreat further and further into his shell, leaning on the bottle to take away the strain. Perry explained, 'There was just so much animosity. I wasn't talking to Steven, we'd go into the studio in shifts. It was hopeless.'

It was plain that Tyler and Perry were pulling in different directions. At the outset of recording the new album and in an attempt to inject some life back into the ailing group and the whole touring experience, they swapped the sanitised stadiums for the clubs, performing as Dr Jones and the Interns. Perry was extremely positive, terming the two gigs they played as among the best they'd ever done. 'We played a show in Boston and another at the Starwood in LA and I realised how much I missed playing those gigs. I could see the people's faces and I was close enough to tell they were enjoying it. We wanted it to turn into a Back To The People tour, clubs and halls. We just did those two gigs before it fell apart and that's where the seed was dropped for me to think about leaving.'

Perry contributed to all the original material on *Night In The Ruts*, except for Tyler's song 'Mia', which was inspired by the birth of his daughter. So keen was Perry that Aerosmith should be able to produce another record to rank with *Rocks* that he worked overtime to get the material in shape and ready for the others to work with. 'For *Night In the Ruts* I had written the basic tracks, the music, with the exception of "Mia", by February 1979, and they were done and cut with as much lead as I could put on without the others in April. We could and should have had that album finished up in a month and out in the summer. It was just taking Aerosmith so long to get the album out and I was so fed up with it because in the mean time all during summer we played a bunch of stadium gigs and couldn't play any new material because it wasn't ready. We had to do the same old songs again and again. We had to cancel the European tour – we were gonna play Knebworth with Led Zeppelin – because we had no album and then we had to blow out an American tour and still the album wasn't out.'

Once more, the problem was Steven Tyler. Always finding it a struggle to write lyrics at the best of times, he was now literally incapable of working on them. Without lyrics and melodies, nothing could be done. The band were marooned in the Mediasound studios, waiting for Tyler to show up and record vocals. When Tyler did arrive, Perry would generally leave the building immediately. His mounting frustration was painfully obvious, complaining bitterly that, 'We kept waiting and waiting for Steven to come up with the lyrics, and finally we had to fill up the record with non-originals. I had all this material that we could have used but Steven wasn't capable.'

At the same time, Joe Perry had other problems to deal with. Aware that he was starting to lose interest in Aerosmith, Leber-Krebs came to him with some quite astonishing news. 'Our managers said I owed the band $80,000 for room-service charges, but if I did a solo record, the advances would wipe it out. They were all fucked up, too. To rub it in, it was just complete bullshit because Aerosmith were making more lucre than God at that point! But I thought I'd make a record to give me an outlet that the band wasn't providing any more.' What were the management's motives at this point? Did Perry really owe them that much and did they really need to recoup the money? It's questionable to say the least. Other forces were surely at work. Perhaps by telling Perry he was in debt, they thought they could bind him to the protective Aerosmith umbrella. If he owed money, the best way to pay it back would be via a mega Aerosmith record and tour just like in the glory days. Yet if that was the case, why suggest a solo record?

The only logical conclusion is that Leber-Krebs felt that Aerosmith weren't long for this world and had concluded that Steven Tyler, for all his considerable qualities, was just too far gone ever to be a credible and successful performer again. Now he was hopelessly unreliable and his future looked bleak. For the sake of their own financial well-being, the management and record company were looking to salvage something from Aerosmith's wreckage, and Perry offered the most promising prospect. Getting him to record a solo album while he was still with Aerosmith provided an ideal opportunity for a little market testing. If the album turned into a hit, perhaps Perry could be prised away from the group and turned into a rock star in his own right.

Perry certainly had enough time on his hands for, outraged by what he saw as yet another betrayal, Tyler responded by retreating further from the studio: 'I would crawl into a little hole with whatever drug I was doing at the time and that was how I lived. I thought it was OK.' Sadly, the rest of the band turned on Perry rather than their fallen leader, Perry remembering, 'While Steven was wasting our time, I'd been working on this solo album on the side and there was a lot of resentment. They'd say I should help Steven, but I'd already done my part, written the tunes, recorded them. What more did they want?' When quizzed on the importance of Perry's forthcoming solo record and its implications for the future of Aerosmith, Tyler replied tartly, 'It's no threat to us at all.'

Eventually, the album was finished for a release in December 1979, nearly six months after it had first been scheduled. Boasting nine songs, there were three covers on there to pad it out as Tyler simply couldn't write any more than six sets of lyrics. With the air of decay that had accompanied its making, *Night In The Ruts* should have been even worse than *Draw The Line*. Paradoxically, it turned out to be a perfectly serviceable, if unremarkable, rock record. Lacking the power and invention of *Toys* or *Rocks*, it remained a solid, sturdy release all the same.

If anything, that demonstrated just how central Perry was to the Aerosmith sound, pointing out that whatever the public perception, it was he, rather than Tyler, who was the most important component in the recording studio. Aerosmith couldn't make a good record without Perry – *Draw The Line* had proved that – but they could make decent records without Tyler – *Night In The Ruts* showed that. Where it was weak was vocally, thanks to Tyler's rapidly deteriorating voice. The album was held together almost exclusively by the power of Perry's guitar work and the strength of his songwriting. Other than the autobiographical lyric from 'No Surprize', Tyler offered nothing of any importance. This did nothing to ease the tensions at work in the band and, in Perry's absence, the tapes were tampered with. Perry pointed out angrily, 'They had Jimmy Crespo re-do a couple of my leads, horns were substituted for a guitar line on "Chiquita" and my guitar parts were mixed down on some of the other songs.'

Even so, Joe came out of the album best of all. On 'Three Mile Smile', all that was worth discussing was the guitar riff, Perry desperately trying to hold it all together. The same was true of

'Cheese Cake' which, along with 'No Surprize' were the only potential Aerosmith classics on the record. The introduction to 'Cheese Cake' borrowed heavily from Zeppelin, but the song still managed to retain its own identify with a breathy sexuality. The cover of The Yardbirds' 'Think About It' was enjoyable for Perry's superb playing, with Hamilton, Kramer and Whitford – none of whom wrote anything for the album – clearly having fun revisiting their roots. 'Bone To Bone' was aggressive for the sake of it, Perry's attack attempting – and failing – to galvanise Tyler into some semblance of a reaction.

The singer just wasn't up to it. Where Perry was defiantly trying to make things happen, attempting to prevent them going under for the third time, Tyler was just too damned tired and too out of his head to make the effort. It was almost as if he was deliberately trying to goad Perry into quitting the band so that he could carry on the Aerosmith name, and earning potential, on his own. Even though by now his entire system was riddled with the effects of his huge chemical intake, it was hard to believe that Tyler couldn't have made a better fist of singing 'Bone To Bone', 'Chiquita' (where the cod-Mexican accent was both ludicrous and distasteful) and 'Think About It', which was plain abysmal. For 'Reefer Head Woman', a slow blues where the band excelled, Tyler was still unimpressive when he should have been in his element, describing the song as 'about a guy with a dope-smoking girlfriend who's upset because he has to drink twice as much to get half as high.' At least he should have been able to identify with the drinking and put a personal stamp on his reading of the lyric, but he just sounded lost and out of place. No one who had been so good three years before could be this bad now, could they? It had to be some kind of bad joke, hadn't it? The only mitigating factor was that Tyler was apparently hooked on opium at the time, possibly the worst substance for one who relied on his voice-box. So if it wasn't deliberately awful singing, then it was hopelessly irresponsible, couldn't-care-less behaviour that caused it. It's hard to know which would be the more aggravating to Perry after he had made such a strong personal commitment to the album.

Geoff Barton noted in *Sounds* that 'Tyler completely refutes the claim that he's too coked up to sing any more.' He pointed to *Night*

In The Ruts being, 'A veritable powerhouse of a platter, umpteen times better than the last studio LP, *Draw The Line*, almost the equal of the definitive *Rocks* . . . raw as a fresh knife wound, it steams along with such rampant power it makes The UK Subs sound like The Commodores . . . gloriously cacophonic . . . an outrageous rendition of The Shangri-La's "Remember (Walking In The Sand)", given the full furious heavy-metal treatment while at the same time not being unfaithful to the song's dramatic pop sensibilities.' David Fricke was a little more circumspect in *Rolling Stone*, but he too had to concede that the album was a partial return to form. 'Aerosmith returns to what it does best, playing America's crass, punkier version of The Rolling Stones . . . but the fact that the finest moments on *Night In The Ruts* sound like inspired out-takes from *Rocks* and *Toys In The Attic* suggests that Aerosmith may be stuck in a hard rock rut of its own . . . 'Mia' is a 'Dream On' clone ruined by a surprisingly lifeless performance . . . now isn't the time for Aerosmith to be lying down on the job . . . when the spirit moves them and the amps are turned up to ten these guys can deliver a paralysing kick. This could have used it.'

So, another million dollars later, Aerosmith surfaced with a record that wasn't quite the resounding endorsement of their quality the band's supporters had been hoping for. Worse was yet to come. The road beckoned again, with the band hitting the tarmac well before the record came out, heeding Tyler's complaint that *Draw The Line* failed because they weren't out there on its release. This time though the band had tempted fate once too often. In Cleveland, all the anger, the frustration and the stupidity that had been pent up over the preceding nine years came spilling out into one huge argument. Tyler remembered, 'Joe was still so mad because it took too long to write the songs for the album. The drugs were really messing me up, I couldn't work. Then there was some stupid argument backstage because Joe's wife threw a glass of warm milk in Tom's wife's face for whatever reason. We were arguing backstage in a trailer. It almost came to blows. We said some horrible things to each other. It was all drug induced.' Though the drugs didn't help, Tyler was evading the issue. The real reason was that he and Perry were simply not sufficiently mature to cope with one another's enormous egos. Perry wanted more songs on the album; Tyler didn't want to give up his cut. Tyler thought Perry couldn't write a lyric to save his life; Perry was sick of waiting for Tyler to prove that he still could. Both wanted centre-stage but they couldn't share any space. Both knew that they needed the other but couldn't bring themselves to admit it. The burning competitive streak that had driven them, the bitter jealousy that made each hate the other's success, the desperate need to outdo the other had finally destroyed their working partnership. Like animals protecting their own space, the only outcome was a vicious fight to the end. Perry knew that Tyler was holding most of the cards, for as far as the public was concerned, Aerosmith without his rubber-lipped public face was utterly unthinkable. Left without any reason to stay following the Cleveland row, Perry quit on the spot, and in fact, for a brief while, it looked as though Brad Whitford would follow him out of the group and into the new Joe Perry Project, but finally he chose to stay. The day after the Cleveland fight, Perry called Hamilton to say, "I just don't think I can go on the road with you guys again. I can't put up with it any more." That was the last official word I said to them.'

Crying over spilt milk seemed a pretty pathetic way for one of America's most successful songwriting partnerships to break up, but if it hadn't happened then, Perry would still have left sooner or later. As far as he was concerned Aerosmith had run its course and couldn't be saved. He told *Sounds* at the time, 'I've played in front of 350,000 people, I've been in a rock movie, I've been to Europe twice, to Japan, I've been through millions of dollars, I've wrecked expensive cars. I've done it all! It got to be so boring. Musically I was a fucking shell. If we did "Dream On", "Back In The Saddle", "Toys In the Attic", "Sweet Emotion" and "Walk This Way", it didn't matter if we sucked. I'm a musician who likes to play and I always enjoyed clubs most. Aerosmith became a big, cumbersome project, it was stifling. It wasn't moving into the 1980s and I got disillusioned.' There were plenty of people who felt the same way for *Night In The Ruts* was only certified as a gold record with 500,000 sales, way down on their previous achievements.

Nevertheless, Aerosmith had to grind on and play the tours that were booked across the US to coincide with the album's release.

Michael Schenker was lined up for Perry's job, but eventually Jimmy Crespo, a twenty-five-year-old from Brooklyn was drafted in to replace him. Within a few days of the tour starting, Tyler collapsed on-stage and all the dates were abandoned.

They booked three different tours in 1980, each of which was cancelled. They then booked a tour of the clubs and managed four shows before calling a halt. Perry's decision to go looked wiser by the day. 'I had to quit because we couldn't get interested in the music. We would drink just to see how much we could consume. That little picture, that little window to what we thought we were about really did suffer in the end and it was best to go.'

Perry was extremely forthcoming about the frustrations that he had had to endure within the band. 'There was a lot of stuff going on. It was amazing, we could sell out anywhere but there was turmoil in the band, we were all really at the edge of our ropes, our nerves were frayed from being on the road so long. The songwriting was dead in the water, though oddly enough, *Night In The Ruts* had some pretty cool Aerosmith songs. But it just felt dead. There was so much shit going on. I wanted to keep playing and return to my roots and the small clubs, a break from what was going on. It was like we were in a tunnel, party after party, always waking up hungover. Every once in a while, it opened up and we were stuck on the stage. It got so insane we started fighting. All the frustrations were being taken out on each other instead of in the normal way through the music, so I left the band. In the great scheme of things, it gave everybody the break that was needed from Aerosmith. But it wasn't done for that, it was done to stop the anger and frustrations from getting too much.'

Tyler's inability to write lyrics was paramount among those frustrations. Joe offered to help out but found himself thwarted by the 'protective stranglehold that Steven had on them'. Tyler wouldn't let anyone else write any words but he couldn't do the job himself, so they reached stalemate. In its turn, that caused terrible logistical problems, Perry explaining, 'Because of the delays, it came down to Aerosmith going out on the road and me havin' to shelve my solo project that was gonna pay off the money I was supposed to owe. Considering what kind of progress I was makin' with Aerosmith, the decision was very easy to make. It was frustration, I felt I'd grown

71

while the rest of the band had stayed in the same place. I needed to freshen up. Y'know, Aerosmith's heavy years didn't last that long. I still have very fresh memories of opening for other acts in small places. But who knows, maybe next year I'll want to go back to the hockey rinks again!'

Joe was absolutely sure that he was following the right path for him, sure that his new found freedom would inspire him musically and might even allow him to break away from the shackles that were his drink and drug dependencies. It was a brave move, for he was stepping into a very uncertain future. With the band breaking up, the obvious conclusion was that since Perry was out, it was he who was at fault. It might be hard to get gigs, it mightn't be so easy to get column inches in the music press, it could be the end of his career. Without the comfort of the Aerosmith brand name, it would certainly be much harder to shift his albums, but Perry maintained, 'If I was in this business for the money, I wouldn't have left Aerosmith. It was something I had to do. And if I had left just because of difficulties between me and Steven, I'd have left the band a long, long time ago. The music started to matter again. In Aerosmith, bits of me came through, watered down. In Aerosmith, there were five guys that gave opinions and it was mutual decisions. We worked together to get a certain goal. I just had more input than they had output to offer, if y'know what I mean. In the Project, it's obviously a direct extension of me, my record will be a little more into R&B than Aerosmith. There are similarities in rhythm but there's more energy track for track. I haven't gotten such a rush from making a record since we did *Rocks* . . . I'm proud of what I did with Aerosmith and it's a drag because it could have gone on to be fucking great but I have no regrets.'

At the start of a new decade, the 1980s, the future of Aerosmith had never looked in such doubt. With their major musical guiding light gone and their charismatic singer a crippled shell of his former self, it looked like one of the foremost bands of the 1970s would die, like their fierce rivals Led Zeppelin, with their decade. For a long while, those predictions looked just about right.

8

WHEN PUSH COMES TO SHOVE

For those with any residual affection for Aerosmith – and that was a dwindling number of people, so thoroughly had their loyalty been abused by the group – the early 1980s were depressing times. Tyler continued to collapse at more or less regular intervals, tours were pulled at the last moment, no new album looked to be forthcoming. Aerosmith looked doomed and many dark rumours began to circulate on the subject of Tyler's own mortality. For a time, it looked as though he might become the next in the long line of rock 'n' roll casualties. Although his rate of chemical ingestion continued unabated, Tyler wasn't going to give up on life that easily for there was still much he wanted to do, even if presently he was in no fit shape to do it. Leber-Krebs and Columbia had hoped that Perry's departure would be the kick in the pants that Tyler required, getting him up and about again, if only to prove to Perry that he didn't need him. Unfortunately, there wasn't sufficient support available to Tyler, for the rest of the band were struggling with their own demons. No one could rouse him from his torpor – Perry had tried on the last record and even he had failed.

Tyler's mental state could scarcely have been eased any when The Joe Perry Project released *Let The Music Do The Talking* in March 1980 to excellent reviews. *Rolling Stone*'s David Fricke reported, 'Perry flexes his muscles like a champ . . . delivers all of the rock 'n' roll moxie that Aerosmith couldn't manage on *Night In the Ruts* . . . the only weak link is singer Ralph Morman, but any singer might have felt intimidated by the locomotive pace and guitar army sound of this album. Any singer except maybe one. If Steven Tyler were here *Let The Music Do The Talking* would probably be the finest record Aerosmith never made.'

Instead of charging back into the studio and recording a powerful, vibrant response to prove that he wasn't dead yet, Tyler sat back and allowed things to carry on sliding. A few months later, he narrowly escaped death in a huge motorbike accident. 'I went flying through the air and hit a tree and got concussion. I almost died. It was much more serious than people thought. I wasn't on drugs either.' The latter part of the statement was made purely for the benefit of the band's booking agents, because he later admitted to having a nose full of coke at the time. Hospitalisation was ideal for Tyler because it enabled him to maintain his drug habit without having to make any connections with the dealers. 'I'd taken my left heel clean off in the smash, so any time I wanted a little more morphine, I'd only gotta ask the doctor. That was a really great time!'

Aerosmith seemed consigned to the history books. Although Hamilton, Whitford and Kramer had all made very valuable contributions to Aerosmith over the years as men, musicians and writers, it had always been Tyler and Perry who were at the helm creatively and commercially. Internal dissension had robbed them of Perry. His own incapacity for work now robbed them of Tyler. With both of the Toxic Twins gone from the scene, the other three were simply incapable of pulling things round for the band. There were back-room boys not leaders, they followed rather than galvanised. So it was that Aerosmith lurched from one disaster to the next.

Brad Whitford finally gave up hope, Tyler recalling, 'Brad quit because he had no patience while I was in hospital. He needed money.' He formed a new group, Whitford/St. Holmes, featuring Derek St. Holmes, singer with Ted Nugent's band. Whitford was speedily replaced by Rick Dufay, who had made a solo album produced by long-time Aerosmith cohort Jack Douglas. Aerosmith were back to the full five again, but there was still nothing for the group to do, especially while Tyler lay in hospital. In fact, there was talk that Crespo, Hamilton and Kramer might form another band, bringing down the final curtain on Aerosmith. That this didn't happen was testament to the incredible determination that could still fire Steven Tyler.

Columbia tried to plug the gap, buying Tyler some recovery time by issuing a *Greatest Hits* collection in 1981, an odd concoction – two tracks from *Draw The Line* and just one from *Night In The Ruts*, their very dodgy Shangri-La's cover – that indicated nevertheless just how great the band had once been. This was one of the factors that finally moved Tyler to take a long hard look at where he and the band were going and to try to rescue something from the situation. Following his accident, Tyler had moved to The Gorham Hotel in Manhattan and was living in squalor. With most of his Aerosmith fortune gone, Tyler would do anything to feed his habit, admitting to stealing during this period.

Much of Aerosmith's decline relates to the questions posed earlier – where do you go once you've reached the top? Now the more pertinent question was what do you do when you've touched bottom? In 1981, Tyler could easily have rolled over and died in a back alley somewhere in New York. The alternative was to get the band back together and start working again. When the reviews for the *Greatest Hits* record ran along the lines of 'Weren't they good and isn't it a shame they're washed up?', the wild arrogance that had been his undoing finally came to Tyler's salvation. The realisation that, in the eyes of the world, Aerosmith were terminally screwed was his wake-up call. Looking back in the 1990s, Tyler explained, 'There are a lot of reasons you get into rock 'n' roll, but at some point you realise it's the music that means the most to you. Without a recovery, we'd have been lost in the shuffle. They'd have looked at one song, "Dream On", and that would have been our legacy. That had to change, I couldn't live with that.' Nor could he live with taking the rap for the band's demise – with Perry having what looked like a reasonably successful solo career, if Aerosmith floundered, the blame would lie with Tyler. If Perry could make a go of things, Tyler had to do likewise.

Not that he suddenly cleaned up his act and went on the wagon. That was still a long way off. Ironically, the introduction of Rick Dufay to the band provided him with another druggie partner to replace Joe. That grabbed Tyler's attention, firing his enthusiasm, for the rest of the band tended to stick to drink. Now that he could take drugs with someone else again, suddenly his enthusiasm for the band returned. On-stage too – on the few occasions that Aerosmith finally got there – Dufay was inspirational, along with the other new boy Jimmy Crespo. For both of them, even though the group was in a very bad way, it still represented a real chance of glory. Neither had tasted real success in the past and Aerosmith still had a comparatively substantial following, so this was the big time. Dufay was so fired up that he even managed to steal the lion's share of the press, something which drove Tyler to distraction. Dufay was regularly sacked by the singer, but each time Tyler went back on his threats, recognising the guitarist's value to him.

Tyler had other worries too. He was all but financially busted, so it was imperative that he got a record out to bring in some cash. In addition, although he was pretty far gone, he was never so far out of it that he missed what was happening among the competition. 'I do remember being laid up on my back in hospital, full of morphine and suddenly seeing this new band, Van Halen, shoot up out of nowhere. I thought, "Jesus, we go out of the spotlight for two minutes and someone else has to come in there".' Van Halen weren't the only new kids on the hard rock block either, for up and coming British bands such as Def Leppard and Iron Maiden were making waves on both sides of the Atlantic. Tyler's market was rapidly disappearing before his eyes and he knew he had to do something about that pretty damn quick.

Therefore 1982 was given over to making a brand new studio album, Aerosmith's first in three years and the first since they'd been shorn of the guitar partnership of Perry and Whitford. The five approached the record with very different sentiments. Although neither Hamilton nor Kramer were averse to the pleasures that went with being in a band like Aerosmith, they had not fallen so far as Tyler or Perry had, and they were in comparatively reasonable shape going into this record. They felt only relief that Aerosmith was finally rolling again at long last, hoping that this might help Tyler get his act together. They'd had to put up with his excesses for so long, they were no longer concerned by them but simply bored, leaving it up to him as to whether he wanted to get help or continue his wayward lifestyle. Dufay was looking forward to the next record, having established himself strongly in Whitford's spot. For him, a place in Aerosmith was wish fulfilment gone mad. This was his big chance.

Jimmy Crespo had similar feelings, though these were tempered by the fact that almost two years on since he joined the band, they'd not recorded a note and he had scarcely played any live shows either. On his arrival back in 1979, he'd heard that Aerosmith were in trouble, but he'd had no inkling that things were as bad as this. Though often tempted to quit, he stayed with the band purely because leaving would have been seen as an admission of failure. Dishevelled and decrepit as Aerosmith were, a good performance by Crespo on an Aerosmith album would act as a powerful calling card in the future. Their name could still open plenty of doors.

For Tyler, this was almost the final throw of the dice. The album had to work if he was to remain a credible force in the hard rock milieu. Anything less and he would be regarded as yesterday's man. With that in mind, he set up camp at New York's Power Station, drafting in Tony Bongiovi as co-producer, hoping to start with a clean slate. This was to prove to be yet another disastrous move. Tyler and Bongiovi had totally conflicting views on the way the record should sound and where the music should be going in the 1980s. Bongiovi was looking towards a crisper, cleaner sound with the crystal production that was becoming the hallmark of records such as *High 'N' Dry* by Def Leppard, a landmark production. Tyler was still stuck in his own groove, trying to repeat the glories of the early days by attempting to recreate sounds that were now out of date. In the end, there was only ever going to be one winner, as Tyler explained, 'We worked with him for four months, early 1982. We didn't get along and I didn't like the way things were going. Jack came back after a while and we finished the record in Miami.'

The return of Jack Douglas to the production console signalled a shift in the band's fortunes. Though they argued, he and Tyler had a real empathy with one another and had long since evolved a successful way of working together. With Aerosmith in such a state of disrepair, Douglas was the ideal controller, knowing full well how to get the best out of Tyler, creating a comfortable, stable working environment in which he felt at home. Perhaps that was the only way in which another Aerosmith record could have been made given the circumstances, yet it had its drawbacks too. Things were too easy, too comfortable, too like the old days. There wasn't enough questioning going on within the band, they were merely making a record for the sake of it. Three long years had passed since *Night In The Ruts* had been recorded, and hard rock had undergone a lot of changes in that time. So too had the studio hardware, a bewildering array of new technology assuming more importance by the day. At no time did the band seem to look at themselves and ask if they were going forward or merely rehashing the music of a previous, redundant decade. When *Rock In A Hard Place* finally came out, it was solid, unspectacular, and dated – a 1978 release would have seen this bunch of recycled Zeppelinisms regarded as a cracker. Four year later it had missed the boat.

Looking for the positives, it was clear that Steven Tyler had started to care about the band once again and was making a thoroughly genuine effort to claw his way back to the top. His performance here was akin to Perry's on *Night In The Ruts*, a last defiant stab at pulling things together, attempting to make the point that he still had something to offer. The irony was that if he had been able to put as much effort into the making of *Night In The Ruts* as he did *Rock In A Hard Place*, maybe the original Aerosmith line-up might have survived and entered the new decade in good shape. As it was, Tyler was left to shoulder the burden alone now, keen to prove to his erstwhile partner that he didn't need him.

The task was beyond him, but it was a brave effort for all that. Still trapped by his addictions, Tyler managed to rise above his infirmities to give a series of surprisingly strong performances. The new guitar partnership of Crespo and Dufay tried hard, but were never as tight as the Perry/Whitford combination, yet their commitment to the cause helped rally Tyler's spirit. Although they are little more than bit players in the Aerosmith story, they deserve a lot of credit for keeping the soul of the group going, and for allowing Tyler and Perry the breathing space they needed from one another. If Crespo and Dufay hadn't helped pull Tyler through the crisis, there's little likelihood that Aerosmith would still be a going concern today. Their performances on *Rock In A Hard Place* at least managed to convey the impression of a band playing with enthusiasm and intent rather than one that had given up the ghost.

However hard they tried though, Tyler was still beyond reach, and while his voice was considerably better than it had been on *Night In The Ruts*, he was a long way from being the bravura singer who had dominated *Rocks*. What did remain intact was Tyler's musical sensibility. He may have been blitzed out of his box for much of the time, but he was not yet a gibbering idiot. He recognised how important this record was to his future and he planned it with great precision. Virtually without exception, the tracks on the new album were based on something that Aerosmith had done particularly well in the past. 'Jailbait' was a 'Toys In The Attic' clone, for instance; the cover of 'Cry Me A River' an echo of the dramatic pop of the Shangri-La's 'Remember (Walking In The Sand)'; 'Rock In A Hard Place' itself could have been an out-take from *Rocks*, allowing Tyler to relax into the sort of heavy blues that he could sing in his sleep. The whole record was a painting-by-numbers exercise that could have been conducted by an Aerosmith tribute band. It was professional, aggressive, funky in some places, woeful in others, tolerably well performed and produced, recognisably Aerosmith. But it was Aerosmith on an off-day, ersatz Aerosmith, sanitised Aerosmith. All the components were in place but there was none of the guts that had made them so exciting six years earlier. In essence, it was a record that you could take or leave, one you could ignore. And that *wasn't* Aerosmith.

For Aerosmith to actually get a record out was a triumph in itself. In terms of their overall history, maybe the album should be looked at a little more indulgently than some of the others, treated as a staging post, a necessary piece of work in the long hard slog to get the band back on its feet. Of course, at the time of its release, it was done no such favours and the reception it received was decidedly frosty. Most cutting was the review from Dennis Hunt in the *Los Angeles Times*. He noted, '*Rock In A Hard Place* simply has neither the power nor the flair of their mid-1970s albums . . . whatever the remedy, it's clear that Aerosmith, regarded by many young fans as a rock 'n' roll dinosaur, needs some rejuvenation.' This was an especially hard review to bear for it was so unerringly accurate.

Aerosmith had become a voice from the past, a golden oldie whose throne had been stolen by bands that had moved the heavy metal genre on to another plane. Led Zeppelin's reputation had survived because they were no longer around to become depressingly pale shadows of their former selves. Tyler was still out there and if there's one thing that committed fans can't stand it's their idols turning into an embarrassment. *Rolling Stones* concurred with the prevailing view that Aerosmith were washed up when J.D. Considine wrote that over the previous three years 'a minor revolution has taken place in heavy rock that has made Aerosmith almost obsolete . . . much of the LP rocks by rote . . . Tyler is unable to energise the slow numbers and they drag interminably.'

The idea that Aerosmith were laughably old-fashioned took further hold a few months after the release of *Rock In A Hard Place*. The release of the movie *This Is Spinal Tap* struck fear in the hearts of hard rock bands everywhere. For Tyler, it had a particularly appalling resonance. 'I was real high at the time and Aerosmith was sinking. We were like a boat going down. And *Spinal Tap* was way too close, way too real. *Rock In A Hard Place* sold like maybe ten copies; Spinal Tap did Stonehenge, and our album cover looked exactly like that. I freaked. I took *Spinal Tap* real personal.' The fictional battles between Tap's leaders David St. Hubbins and Nigel Tufnel, sparked by the ubiquitous 'rock wives' must have struck a further chord. Just as Tap disintegrated, so too had Aerosmith. Was Tyler going to be relegated to peddling his old hits in Japan?

Rock In A Hard Place wasn't quite *Shark Sandwich*, though 'Bitch's Brew' should clearly have been on *Smell The Glove*. There were other similarly crass moments but they totally lacked the mocking humour of yesteryear, so that Tyler no longer looked like a mischievous lech, but more like a dirty old pervert. That was also true of 'Jailbait', the fast and furious opener fuelled by squealing guitars that tried to launch the album as *Toys In The Attic* had been launched seven years before. Lacking wit, this vaguely misogynistic twaddle had no real character, speed and bluster trying to mask the void at its heart. The sensitive side also fell flat. 'Prelude To Joanie' used a vocoder to intone some poetic drivel that was so dismal, even Jon Anderson wouldn't have used it on *Tales From Topographic*

Oceans. Luckily, the vocoder rendered much of the lyric incomprehensible, but in a moment of absolute madness the original felony of its composition was compounded by having the words printed on the sleeve. This merely proved that even when you knew what Tyler was saying, it was still incomprehensible.

It was sad that 'Prelude To Joanie' was so unremittingly awful for the next track, 'Joanie's Butterfly', was by far the best song on the record. Tyler later remarked that the title related to a sex aid, but there was no sense of that in the lyric. Opening in folksy fashion, the treatment was light, delicate and rather experimental. It showed Tyler starting to get a grip on himself and his music once again, the band employing inventive instrumental touches and some of their trademark vocal harmonies. Technically, Tyler was beginning to approach his best once more, but emotionally he was still empty. His performance on 'Lightning Strikes' was solid and controlled but utterly soulless. Even when the Richie Supa-penned lyric spoke of 'combat zones' and 'rivals', offering him the chance to return fire on Perry, the spark was gone. Much the same was true of the bar-room trawl that was 'Cry Me A River'. The first verse was promising – Tyler might not have been Julie London, but at least he was stamping some personality on the song. Then it all went horribly wrong, crashing into an awful, stupid metal arrangement that exposed all the flaws in his voice and completely destroyed the affecting atmosphere of self-pity. Vocally, the only evidence that Tyler still had something new to offer came in the funky 'Bolivian Ragamuffin' which rolled along on that characteristic Aerosmith swing. Rhythmically exciting, it was driven by Tyler's highly distinctive phrasing, suggesting that he and the band might still have a future. Those few compensations aside, it was hard to disagree with *Q*'s retrospective summing up of the album: 'paper thin'. The American public felt much the same. It reached number thirty-two and didn't even achieve gold status, the first time that had happened in eight years.

If it accomplished little else, at least *Rock In A Hard Place* proved that Aerosmith were still around and that there might be life in the old dog yet. The next item on the agenda was to convince concert promoters that they could be relied upon to put on a good show and, more importantly, complete a tour. Over the previous three years,

Tyler and his cohorts had done their level best to upset anybody and everybody connected with the record industry. Columbia had all but given up on them and promoters everywhere were tired of their unreliability. If Aerosmith were serious about continuing, they needed to win those people back over to their side. Tyler went on a charm offensive, giving a variety of wide-eyed and highly disingenuous interviews to the press. Try this for size: 'let's take heroin for example. Even before I tried it – I've snorted a few times in my life – the rumours were Tyler was a junkie. How ridiculous. I don't like the stuff because it's too easy to get caught up in.' Or how about: 'I'll do a line of coke any time so long as it's not before I go on-stage. When that curtain goes up and I hear the crowd, the last thing I need is coke. I'm that kind of animal, I get off on the crowd so much, there's moments on stage when I'm almost stoned, like lucid dreaming, I don't even know where I am half the time.' Then again: 'I've gone on-stage quite inebriated. If I have interviews to do before I go on, I'll lean on the booze.' Quite inebriated? Tyler was used to going on stage so drunk he could barely stand up. These were comments designed to woo wavering promoters, but even then, he was forced to say, 'Have I straightened out? Never! Some people dig that, they think it's neat I can be a bad boy and still have a career.'

Clearly Steven hadn't noticed that he no longer had much of a career. The venues were getting smaller, the halls emptier, the interest in his escapades dwindling. Tyler was impervious to much of this because he still had little idea what was going on in his life. Reflecting later, he recalled, 'The road manager would come backstage and say, "Fine, drink all you want. Just go on the stage, don't cancel the show".' That was great for an alcoholic to hear, the perfect place to be; liquor flowed backstage. I don't blame anybody. Four rehab centres for drug abuse later, I've been able to take a long hard look at my behaviour, but back then it was just great.'

On the few occasions that he did notice how far down Aerosmith were heading, he must have drawn consolation from the fact that Joe Perry's career was circling the U-bend too. Perry was so out of things that he didn't even realise Aerosmith had released the *Greatest Hits* package until he was asked to sign it by a fan in a supermarket! Musically, the promise of *Let The Music Do The Talking* had evaporated and he released two further solo offerings to diminishing returns, in spite of a number of encouraging reviews such as this one for *I've Got The Rock 'n' Rolls Again* by *Sounds'* Xavier Russell: 'Once again the man has come up with a few gems . . . "Buzz Buzz" could easily become a top ten smash [if the record company pushed it].' Just as the fans were ignoring Aerosmith, Joe Perry was also way down on the list of promotional priorities. After *Let The Music* had sold 250,000 copies, his third offering, *Once A Rocker*, shifted just 40,000 units. Pretty soon, the newly divorced Perry was broke and stuck in a Boston boarding house, finally ending up sleeping rough on his manager's couch. The split had been a total failure for him, even if he had been reunited with Brad Whitford after Whitford/St. Holmes disbanded.

Back at the ranch, Tyler and the boys were going through the motions in city after city, Steven occasionally brightening the show by keeling over or falling off the stage. Things had reached such a point that he finally admitted, 'I miss Joe and the fans miss Joe. I look over at the other guys and they're really good but I just know something's missing. I miss Joe so much.' Sounds like a cue for a reunion . . .

9

ROLL UP, ROLL UP FOR THE RESURRECTION SHUFFLE

Ever since Perry had quit the band back in 1979, rumours had surfaced from time to time to the effect that he was ready to rejoin forces with his former partners in crime. For the most part these were mere pipe-dreams, for the rift that existed was just too deep to be brushed away in a matter of months. That said, other rumours suggesting that should Tyler and Perry ever meet again it would lead to a fight to the death, were equally off the mark. In fact as Perry confessed, 'Steven and I had been talking on the phone over the three years but we never told anybody about it.' A strong bond of friendship remained between them and the eventual four-year estrangement had given sufficient breathing space for them to forget many of the worst times and remember the better moments.

If Aerosmith had still been having hit records, or if Perry had eclipsed his work in the band as a solo star, there would have been no chance of reconciliation. As it was, everyone was down on their luck, facing a brick wall where the future was concerned. An Aerosmith reunion, even though it was anything but a sure-fire success, was at least a more attractive proposition than continuing as they were. Perry was now a nobody, yet few wanted to see Aerosmith without him and Whitford, for that would no longer be the authentic Aerosmith. There was only one conclusion to be drawn, and Perry's new manager Tim Collins busied himself drawing it up. He took Perry and Whitford along to a couple of Aerosmith shows, including one at the Worcester Centrum, having previously dragged Tyler to some Joe Perry Project club gigs. Having Whitford on hand was vital for Perry's self-esteem for it prevented him looking like a desperate outsider trying to force his way back in. Musically too, Whitford was crucial, for as Perry pointed out, 'Brad always put a different slant on our music and always shook up my outlook on things.' Nervous at meeting his old colleagues and keen to impress with his macho antics, Tyler produced some heroin before the show, promptly collapsing on stage midway through the gig. It was apparent that any reunion would take some sensitive handling but, following intensive discussions, the infamous five felt they had little alternative but to give it one more shot. Tyler's version of events was, naturally, rather more melodramatic than a gradual drift towards the inevitable: 'I heard Joe was going to join Alice Cooper's band in 1984. I got riled, called him and said, "What the fuck is this?"'

Like the good emotional invalids that some of them were, they chose to blame everyone but themselves for their earlier demise, Perry pointing out, 'Now Brad had left and Aerosmith wasn't going anywhere I felt I could talk to them. I realised I didn't hate them. It was the shit that separated us, like being led around by our management or chasing off after our dealers. We gathered around a table in Tom's house and decided to change the structure from the ground. So that meant getting rid of the record company, managers, everybody. We swept it clean. I don't think CBS wanted us back anyhow, they'd had so many bad experiences.'

Stripping away the structures that had led to their downfall was to be helpful in the long term but for the time being, it proved that they had yet to develop the inner strength necessary to confront their own demons. Perry had begun the long haul back: 'I'd given up drinking in summer of 1983, which wasn't easy,' but Tyler still continued to live the rock star life to the full.

Reforming the band was one thing. Ridding themselves of the now superfluous Crespo and Dufay was another. Their passing was eased by the fact that neither could stand being around Tyler any more, Crespo suffering particularly at his hands for the heinous crime of not being Joe Perry. The band had tried writing together late in 1982 prior to making a new album, but Tyler and Crespo had nothing to say to one another. The choice was a stark one – either Crespo and

Dufay left of their own volition, or the band would fold. In April 1984, their choice was revealed when a statement issued to the press informed the world that Joe Perry and Brad Whitford had rejoined Aerosmith.

Never a band renowned for their maturity, under the influence of new manager Tim Collins, Aerosmith made one of their better decisions. Embarking on a huge Back In The Saddle tour that criss-crossed America, they played a series of shows in smaller theatres and clubs. Not only did this allow them to break themselves in as a band once more before tackling the recording studio, it allowed the fans that had stood by them to catch a glimpse of the guys close up, something denied them for almost a decade. Brad Whitford both understood and accepted the need for such a show of strength: 'It was humbling. Before the split we'd been selling out stadiums but on the Back In The Saddle tour it was strictly clubs and no company support. We couldn't complain, we'd let a lot of people down and we had to win that trust back.'

Attacking the tour with the best of motives, intending to stay straight and work hard, there were still plenty of times when they failed to live up to the lofty ideals, Tyler falling off a Los Angeles stage in June for instance, repeating the process in Springfield, Illinois. The latter gig was abandoned, Tim Collins arranging for free albums to be mailed to the disgruntled ticket holders. For Collins, that was among the least of his problems, terming the whole tour, 'Pure guerrilla warfare. They were still signed to Columbia at that point but no one wanted to speak to us. They would only talk to Leber-Krebs, who had the production contract for seven more albums. So we said, "Fuck it, we'll go on the road and get out of this contract." We made up a bogus corporation for each show so that the money couldn't be taken by creditors. There was officially no Aerosmith at that time. And the guys were road animals, they needed the focus to get them back together. And they needed money real bad.'

The band had elected to replace Leber-Krebs with Tim Collins as part of their attempt to pull everything up by the roots. However, since Aerosmith were signed to Leber-Krebs rather than Columbia and since Columbia were anticipating a further batch of records out of that deal, this was causing real difficulties. Ultimately they got out of the deal in typical Aerosmith fashion. They ignored the realities and carried on playing gigs. They refused to record for Leber-Krebs and issued a volley of law suits. Freed from their clutches while the cases worked their way through the legal system, they soon found that Columbia were only too pleased to see the back of them. For the first time since Clive Davis had seen them at Max's in New York more than a decade ago, Aerosmith were without a deal.

For many bands, especially bands that had seen better and, according to many, perhaps their best days, that would have seemed a terrifying prospect, but for Aerosmith it looked like a whole new opportunity. Tyler summed up the prevailing philosophy: 'If you're afraid to take a risk, OK, stay there baby. But if you take a risk, two things can happen. People will laugh at you or you'll be way ahead of everybody. And if that's what you're in it for, you gotta take that risk. I've seen too many fuckin' people who are dead before they're alive. They don't want to take a risk. They are B and C personalities, happy enough to work in a laundromat, God bless 'em, but I gotta tell you, there are a lot more rewards out there.'

The reward this time came by way of Geffen Records. Their A&R man John Kalodner – that's him in the wedding dress in the 'Dude (Looks Like A Lady)' video – felt that with the classic line-up back in harness, it was worth taking a $7,000,000 gamble on their future. He'd been a fan in the 1970s and had seen the band enough times this time around to know they could still cut it. There were plenty of other observers who endorsed his view, people who sensed that Aerosmith might just be on the way back. The *Los Angeles Times* recorded this highly enthusiastic verdict on an August show in San Diego's Golden Hall: 'Aerosmith performs with the passion of men who've learned their lessons well . . . none of this was lost on the 3,000 who packed The Golden Hall. They stood on chairs, rapt and responsive, from start to finish as Aerosmith delivered its fierce, sardonic anthems. Aerosmith may have trouble withstanding its inner turbulence, but so far its best music is standing the test of time.'

Checking into Fantasy Studios in Berkeley, the band embarked on yet another make-or-break project. Their collective resolution to play it straight went out of the window amid the sheer grinding tedium that attends a studio recording. In 1985 the health of the band was still highly questionable. Industry rumours had it that Tyler was still an alcoholic and a heroin user, Perry had quit booze but was still a junkie, Kramer and Whitford had the same attitude to drinking as the singer, and Tom Hamilton had a problem with cocaine. In that sense, little had changed since the downwards spiral had begun in 1978 with *Draw The Line*. All that could be said in their favour was that the atmosphere and the attitude that surrounded them was considerably improved. That came through on the record, but then so too did the drunken haze. Ted Templeman, one of the hottest producers in the game, did his best to marshal the troops into some kind of shape, but much of the inspiration got lost in the fog. Like *Rock In A Hard Place* before it, *Done With Mirrors* was filled with good intentions that simply failed to translate. Like its predecessor too, it was a record that had to be made to flush out the Aerosmith system and leave them free to go on with the rest of their career.

It had been six years since these five had assembled in the studio. It takes a lot to recover from that kind of break, particularly when so much had been experienced in the interim. They were changed men in many respects and it would have been foolish to expect them to come back with a classic first time out. There again, the fans might have expected something a little better than what they received. Perry was honest enough to own up to their culpability. 'It came out in 1985 when we were still doing drugs and it was a disaster. Our attitude was wrong, it wasn't just the drugs. You get yourself in a box and you can't see out of it.'

One far-sighted attitude that was adopted was in the crediting of songs to the band as a whole rather than the individuals. Committed to giving things the very best chance of working out, they sensibly reasoned that if the publishing was split equally, there would be fewer disagreements over money and fewer fights over who got credit for what. If they could take fragile egos out of equation, the prospects for success were instantly much brighter. Things could scarcely have opened in finer style than 'Let the Music Do The Talking', the old Perry tune dusted down for the new album, after having proved itself as a live favourite on the recent tour. Feisty, punchy, gutsy, it had everything 'Jailbait' had lacked, underlining that Aerosmith was something much more than the mere sum of its constituent parts. Like so many really good bands, they had a style, a chemistry that could only be captured with the right line-up at the right time. Perry couldn't capture it alone, Aerosmith couldn't make it work without him. 'Let The Music Do The Talking', surely now their motto, was an anthem for a new era, an emphatic statement that 'we're back!' It was equally promising that Tyler had allowed the album to open with a song so clearly identified with Perry, suggesting that the tantrums were a thing of the past.

'Shame On You', a classic Stonesy blues, was another step in the right direction. Despite the cloudiness and the cobwebs that still cloaked them, it was apparent that they were a band once more, unified and moving in one clearly defined direction. The downside was that the performance was sloppy and the song could have been so much better realised. While that might have been engaging in 1976, in the post-Leppard world of 1985, it wasn't good enough any more. 'Shela' was a similar Aerosmith on auto-pilot job, the band enjoying recording but simply chucking everything in there and hoping that something good might come out of the mix. It was a confusion that coloured 'The Reason A Dog' too, an unconvincing cross between rocker and ballad. Templeman's production attempted to elevate it to the required modern standard, but the group seemed unsure whether to head for their roots or forge out in a new direction. It was apparent that once again, simply cutting a record was a triumph in itself this time around, but songs like this made observers wonder if they had any real conception of where to go next time. The fear in the lyric – the 'hold your tongue' line – reinforced the message of the title track: this reunion is a fragile thing, take things slowly, handle with care. It felt as if Tyler and Perry were too scared to argue, to let rip, to let the sparks fly in case it broke up the band once more. By restraining themselves, they were denying the band the motivating force that had driven it in the past. 'She's On Fire' was a case in point, Aerosmith relaxing in the comfort zone, dated but easy on the ear, posing no new questions for them.

'My Fist Your Face' was one of the few songs that belied that impression. Like the CD closer 'Darkness' – inexplicably left off the vinyl version – this really did sound like a band with a mission. The former had a nice vibe to it, a power, an aggression that was lacking on other songs, allowing Tyler to recapture that sexual swagger even though his voice was still a little too rough really to carry it off. 'Darkness' was the most progressive and influential piece on view, a real pointer for the future. Its menacing strut caught the swing that a band only achieves when it locks together after years of experience and is confident with its own abilities. 'The Hop' showcased similar intent, and the funky, chunky rhythm of 'Gypsy Boots' pointed out that they weren't ready to be pensioned off.

On release, the album scraped a gold disc, a minor improvement on *Rock In A Hard Place*, but still a major disappointment. Aerosmith obviously had a lot of fences still to mend with their loyal supporters. They set about it the only way they knew how, by going back on the road. They were fortunate that a number of bands had recreated an interest in the rock genre – Motley Crue, Def Leppard, Ratt, Van Halen and AC/DC were all doing very good business at the time, getting people back out to the gigs. If any band could capitalise on that, it was Aerosmith, for as Perry pointed out, 'We'd helped pioneer arena rock – Van Halen made such a clean sweep because we weren't around any more.'

If only life were that simple. Within months, Aerosmith had fallen out of the saddle again, physical wrecks incapable of finishing a show, Tyler leading the way in that department: 'I should be dead. There were enough toxins in me to kill ten people. I was the most obnoxious creep. People would always tell me what a jerk I was when I was high. I paid the price.' A halt was called to the touring cycle. Joe Perry was left to explain away the fine mess they'd gotten themselves into: 'We were still dabbling, trying to control the drugs, but we realised we had to change after *Done With Mirrors*. It didn't work, so we had to do something drastic.'

10

HERE COMES THE CAVALRY

With the Done With Mirrors tour prematurely aborted, the prospects for the future looked bleak once again. That was only further underlined when Columbia pieced together a new Aerosmith release in May 1986. *Classics Live!*, a hotchpotch of recordings found in the vaults, reached number eighty-four, a pretty dismal return for what was an admittedly uneven and poorly planned record, Jimmy Crespo touching up some of the material in the studio while Aerosmith's own participation wasn't invited. *Q* remarked that this and its sister album, *Classics Live II*, released a year later, but this time with the assistance of the band, should be approached with caution: 'Anyone curious to hear a band attempt to play good rock 'n' roll on scary drugs is welcome to invest.' *Vox* took an alternative view and felt that the recordings caught 'a stadium band at their powerhouse peak.' What wasn't in dispute was the fact that Aerosmith's popularity continued to plummet unchecked.

Ironically in the face of such disarray, 1986 was the year when they finally turned the corner, launching the comeback that turned them into the multi-platinum selling act of today. The first, and most unlikely, source of salvation came in the form of the rap act Run DMC. Back in 1986, rap was still very much a ghettoised form of music with virtually no access to the mainstream, but for those in the know, it was clear that this was the coming thing. Pretty soon, rap was going to take the musical world by storm, so Aerosmith becoming associated with its vanguard was a prescient commercial move.

Perry remembers, 'We were still out on tour with *Done With Mirrors*. I'd heard of rap 'cos my fourteen-year-old was playing it all the time. Then I saw an article in *Rolling Stone* about Run DMC, where Rick Rubin said they really liked "Walk This Way". A little while later he called up and asked if we wanted to sit in on the recording, so we flew to New York and did the session. It was pretty cool. We weren't sure that it was going on the *Raising Hell* record at first but it went so well. Then they wanted a video, we got on it, and next thing we know it's this huge single. The video was really good with the smashed wall breaking down the barriers between black and white. It was the first time rap had gotten some music behind it, it had been a kick drum with scratching items over it. Now you get all kinds of electric guitars over it. I think it made rap more accessible, gave it a broader audience. I just wish it had brought the stadium audiences together.'

If any hard rock tune might have been written with the emergence of rap in mind, it had to be 'Walk This Way'. That huge, simple funked-up riff was ideal tape-loop fodder, its dance beat as irresistible in 1986 as it had been in 1976. Brad Whitford was especially pleased with the collaboration even though he, like Kramer and Hamilton, didn't get to play on the re-make or appear in the video: 'When so much rock 'n' roll comes from black guys playing the blues it's always disappointed me that Aerosmith attracts a mainly white audience. I suppose there are bigots on both sides but hopefully us doing that with Run DMC chipped away at a few prejudices.'

Great song though it was, and superbly as Run DMC had reworked it, it was probably the video that finally propelled the single into the upper reaches of the charts on both sides of the Atlantic – number four in the US, eight in the UK. It wasn't the most subtle piece of work – music breaking down walls that existed between black and white – but there were enough moments of humour in there to show that Tyler could still steal a scene from anyone. The look on his face at the start as he opened his mouth to sing and instead heard Run DMC blasting out from the PA was priceless, as was his synchronised dancing. He wasn't going to be upstaged by anyone, but he was gracious enough to accept the huge push this gave to their ailing career, saying, 'That opened the door to a younger and different audience; there are a lot of black kids now who know Aerosmith because of Run DMC.' It also gave Aerosmith its first real exposure on MTV, something that would prove to be central to their renaissance.

Most important of all, after the damp squib of the Mirrors tour, it gave the group, fans, management and record company fresh hope. It was all the more important that they should now take the drastic action of which Perry had spoken. Nobody in Aerosmith would have ever had the audacity to call themselves an angel. They all had plenty of problems and they all had to lean on some substance or another to get them through. That had taken its toll and their widely varying output since they'd reached a peak with *Rocks* testified to this. Everyone had to shoulder some of the blame but, as the guy who had to out-do all the rest and as the guy who was causing more trouble than all the others put together, it was time for Steven Tyler particularly to sort himself out. An on-stage collapse wasn't quite the regular feature of the act that it had been, but in the multi-million dollar world of rock 'n' roll in the 1980s, pulling out of one show was still one too many. His irresponsible behaviour could no longer be tolerated. Once the Done With Mirrors tour had finally disintegrated, Tim Collins called the band together and allowed everyone to let rip at Tyler, hammering him into submission with a few home truths. It remains one of the most emotionally charged meetings in the band's history and Tyler still bears the scars, complaining, 'I'm still just a little bitter about that, because there were guys in the room who had problems of their own telling me how fucked up I was.'

Perry's assertion that the prevailing attitude to drink and drugs was 'it's okay, I can handle it', illustrated that they were men labouring under the typical delusion of the addict. Anyone from outside could see that they couldn't handle it, that they were running out of goodwill and that if they didn't clean up now and start to work properly once again, they were doomed.

Tyler held the key and so he was packed off for some psychiatric treatment to get to the root of his addiction. He was forced to relive the countless humiliations that he'd gone through because of his addictions, and came out the other end determined to kick his habits. Sensibly, he and Collins insisted that if he was going to clean himself up, the others needed to do likewise. If Tyler returned fit and healthy to a dressing-room full of Jack Daniels and cocaine, maybe his renewed self-control wouldn't be enough to keep him on the straight and narrow.

Block-booking rooms in a detoxification and rehabilitation centre in Pennsylvania, the five all began the long haul back towards normality. Recovery from any addiction can be a long, harrowing experience. Aerosmith were luckier than some. They could afford the very best treatment, and they had a worthwhile goal to aim for – a resurrected career and a pot of cash. Even so, that doesn't make the physical and mental trials of withdrawal and rehabilitation any easier, so they deserve great credit for emerging from the treatment centre straightened out and ready to roll once more. Tom Hamilton was grateful that things had at last been resolved, saying, 'We had the need to put the band together and prove to ourselves, the public and the industry that we weren't yesterday's men. We were lucky in that we had someone like Tim Collins with the balls to make us face facts we'd otherwise have ignored.'

By its very nature, the treatment caused them to reflect on their hedonistic behaviour of the previous fifteen years and it was this that caused much of the pain. Tyler was especially hard on himself, but then he had good reason to be: 'My wife and I lost a child. Because of the head space we were in, we chose to abort. I would never do that today.' Not only had they lost that child, but Tyler himself had missed out on the childhood of another young girl. Way back when Aerosmith were at their peak, Tyler had his pick of America's most nubile young women. He had a brief fling with Bebe Buell, a model and famous 'rock chick', a prototype Patsy Kensit who was also involved with the likes of Elvis Costello and Todd Rundgren. She gave birth to a daughter of uncertain paternity. Tyler confessed later, 'I'm sad to say that when I met Bebe I was so busy and in the throes of my drug addictions, caught up in the wheels of the machine that I wasn't sure whose child Liv was until I saw her at a Todd Rundgren show. And I started crying and said, 'Oh my God.' I tried to hold back the emotions a little but apparently Liv couldn't help but see how much kin she and I were.' She was brought up as Liv Rundgren in the belief that Todd was her father. Now of course, she's making her own waves in the film industry as a highly acclaimed actress, happily carrying her real father's surname.

Aware that he couldn't adequately atone for the sins and omissions of the past, Tyler set himself to face the future. He'd retained that characteristic arrogance but he soon betrayed the religious connotations of the recovery programme when he proclaimed, 'I think God gave us a gift and this band is bigger and better than anything that's out there. The public has the right to see it.'

Joe Perry was a little more realistic about things, especially his own behaviour and the powerful attractions of the life he'd lived. 'I'd probably do it again if I had the chance. I don't regret anything. It just got the better of us. I can't sit back and advise people not to do that. I did it and I wasn't going to take advice from anybody. If they do it and live through it, more power to them. I got sober through myself and outside factors. We've learned a lot of real hard lessons. Trends come and go all the time. You can live the rock 'n' roll lifestyle on the stage but off it you gotta do what's right for you.'

Their rehabilitation had given them a second chance in life but musically they were on to their final shot. Aerosmith's revival, their second coming, had been regularly trailed throughout the decade but the band had never really looked like living up to the hype. In 1987, there was no choice. Another failure and that would definitely be the end. In the past, that kind of pressure would have ripped the group apart or at the very least driven them into the arms of a dope dealer or a liquor store. At long last they now had the inner strength to cope with what was expected of them and the intelligence not to hide behind the corporate stupidity of the music business. They relied on one another, not on drink. The writing process saw them heading out – very nervously – into uncharted waters, as Tyler explained, 'One of the big hurdles was "will I still be creative if I don't smoke a joint first?" That was kinda scary. Then you find you can actually remember things without a tape recorder! It used to be tearing your hair out and spending more money on drugs than on the recording procedure. When you get rid of it all, the glaze, the music just comes. You don't realise how much time and energy you've been wasting, coppin' dope, talkin' to the connection, going' to the john.'

One thing that the Done With Mirrors tour had shown them once and for all was that the rock audience had changed for good. Ten years before, a hard rock show would have been attended by a pretty rough crowd, about ninety-five per cent of which would have been male. With the advent of Van Halen, Bon Jovi, Def Leppard and the glam-metal bands, girls had been wooed to the shows and once there, they were treated like people rather than sheep to be herded from one part of a stadium to the next. Gig-going was a considerably more punter-friendly experience than it had been in the days that had spawned Altamont and Cincinnati. You could get something to eat and drink and you could enjoy yourself without having to worry about the junkies who might be sitting shooting up behind you. In the 1980s, rock was cleaned up and sanitised, and a lot of people enjoyed it all the more for that. Managers, bands and agents loved the change in culture too for these new, improved facilities helped them justify the ever-escalating price of the concert ticket. In turn, that created an ever-more élite crowd, one that was more affluent and merchandise-hungry. Such crowds were more manageable than before but they were far more demanding too, insisting that they should get value for their money. No more falling off-stage . . .

From Aerosmith's perspective, that required some fundamental changes to be made to their music and particularly their lyrics. In the old days, they were all about taking a macho stance, exploiting an aggressive, misogynistic sexuality that treated women as objects to be played with and then discarded. That kind of idea might have gone down well enough in front of a crowd of teenage boys, but now, with an older crowd and with girls taking up a greater share of the audience, it was time that Aerosmith ditched their 1960s attitudes and woke up to the new realities of the 1980s. Tyler's initial pronouncements didn't bode well, pointing out. 'It used to be the only girls at our shows were the ones who came to blow us on the bus. Now thousands of sixteen-year-old girls are there. So now you know why we're still together!'

Fortunately, Joe Perry had a slightly firmer grip on the world, making the astute comment, 'Heavy metal bands have taken the sex out of rock music. They sing about it but they don't project it, it's all show and no go.' To rob Steven Tyler of his use of sexual innuendo would have been to neuter him musically, taking away one of

Aerosmith's greatest weapons. What was required was a subtle shift in viewpoint and in tone. Where his lyrics had been 'good ol' boys together' fare, coarse and purely masculine, they now needed to trade on a different kind of sexuality. Tyler was still attractive to the fans, his greatest talent was as a flirt, coming on to every girl in the auditorium. Now though he had to play on the irony of the situation, laughing at himself and his caricature role as a great rock stud, removing the threat of violence that had always been hinted at in the past.

It was a tough job, calling on him to reassess his motives, forcing him to write in a completely different way. To assist with this transition, he and the band called in some help: 'As a lyricist I wait until the last minute to finish a lot of things. Joe's got all these licks and I put something with them to give us a shell and we go into the studio with a shelf full of unfinished bits and pieces that make up the album. Then I have to write a whole lot of lyrics, which drives me fucking crazy. So, with everything else that was going on this time, rather than have that extra pressure, I asked John Kalodner at Geffen if he knew anyone who could help. He suggested Desmond Child who he knew from the band Rouge in New York. Desmond flew into Boston and we got to know each other. We took the attitude of "Let's write ourselves a hit" and we came up with "Angel". The next day I was four hours late into the studio and they had "Heart's Done Time", so it was obvious that Desmond's real good. He helped me keep up with Joe 'cos he's got a million licks. I worked with Holly Knight too; I asked her to help with "Rag Doll" and we fixed it in five minutes, she picked things out, the little extra it needed.'

The introduction of these new writers was extremely important and indicative of a major change in attitude within the band. In the past, cover-versions aside, virtually all their material was self-penned with the very occasional piece of assistance from close friends. Bringing in a hired gun like Desmond Child – then on the crest of a wave following his vital role in the Bon Jovi success story – served notice to all in the industry that they were taking this new record very seriously indeed. The value of these new interlopers was apparent on even the most cursory run through of the album. The album opener 'Heart's Done Time' was a case in point, tighter, harder, bigger, with not an ounce of spare flesh on it. A perfect example of pristine mid-1980s hard-edged pop, it was clear that Aerosmith had absorbed the nuances of the current music scene from their accomplices and had learnt many lessons from it.

They were further aided by their astute choice of producer. Bruce Fairbairn had won his spurs as producer of *Slippery When Wet* for Bon Jovi, a multi-million-selling album that broke the band worldwide. Perry admitted, 'We'd thought of using him for *Done With Mirrors* but we liked what Ted Templeman had done going all the way back to Montrose. Going with Bruce this time was a smart move because we wanted a coach, someone to get involved with everything we were doing and who would understand the songs. He's got a good background, he's still a musician. On top of all that, it was nice to be in Vancouver to record, it kept us out of trouble. We worked twelve or fourteen hours a day. There was no rock scene that you felt you had to be part of.' Maybe that was part of Tim Collins' master-plan, sticking the band well away from the temptations of Los Angeles or New York, still uncertain that they had put their hell-raising days behind them.

The choice of Fairbairn was inspirational, 'Heart's Done Time' testifying to his value, not only in marshalling the sound but in creating a highly charged and highly creative atmosphere in the studio. Tyler remembered, 'We just had a rave-up at the start; we were rehearsing and Bruce just said, "Wait, that's great, do it again!" Joe got the feedback going and the thing sounded like whales, so we recorded that at an aquarium. Those kind of things, we wouldn't have tried them in the past but Bruce wanted to try different things and that gave the record a nice feel.'

The album went under the title *Permanent Vacation*, as good a summing up of the Aerosmith philosophy as you could find. The title track was a delight and a wonderful tonic for those with the band's best interests at heart. A cool, relaxed atmosphere ran through it from the Caribbean feel of the introduction through to the witty quote from the Calypso classic 'Yellow Bird' at the end. Lyrically, too, it was encouraging for it concentrated on their need to get out of the fast lane and to avoid burn out. So relaxed were they, they reached back to their 1960s roots with Motown being an especially strong influence. 'Girl Keeps Coming Apart' was based on an R&B feel, Kramer hitting the blue-eyed soul beat, the song motoring along in a way reminiscent of 'Keep On Running' by The Spencer Davis Group.

That song was indicative of their rapid evolution. A Chandleresque tale of a hooker, it had the misogynist overtones of old, but Tyler was obviously trying to change things around. No one but Tyler could have got away with the song, particularly the last 'ace in the hole' line that dripped with sexual implication. However, rather than being sung in the vicious, sadistic tones that might have accompanied it on *Rocks*, Tyler now let rip with a leering laugh that let everyone in on the joke. It wasn't perfect, but it was a start. The same was broadly true of 'Hangman Jury', but this time the singer had been betrayed by 'his' woman, something that he would never have conceded possible first time around.

Musically, 'Hangman Jury' was one of the most intriguing songs on view. A delta blues, it created vivid pictures in the mind, Perry noting, 'It was the only thing where, when we were arranging it, we had a visual image of it as well as a sound image. It was just a shack in the middle of the plains, a rocking chair on the porch, the wind blowing the tumbleweeds.' A lovely, jangly melody coloured the piece beautifully, Tyler proving himself to be back on the very best form. There were similar pieces on show such as 'St. John'. A real cool blues with a dark, brooding film-noir feel, Tyler added a superb vocal, railing against the rise of TV evangelism. 'Simoriah' on the other hand was a blast of Monkees-style pop, the cover of 'I'm Down' was a pure blast, a band enjoying themselves and delighted to be back in the studio.

For Aerosmith purists, though it was great to have them back and on top form, there were a few causes for concern. 'Magic Touch', which employed Fairbairn's trademark huge sound, dwarfed everything, running up the curtain on a new ultra-hard rocking Aerosmith. A key question needed to be asked – where had Aerosmith's love of the blues gone? 'Hangman's Jury' aside, there was little authentic here. 'Magic Touch', characterised as it was by strong performances from all, was very Bon Jovi – the 'Livin' On A Prayer' chorus was readily apparent – albeit a far heavier variant.

They sounded like a band enthused by themselves again, a band making up for lost time, but also a band that knew precisely what they wanted. It seemed clear that Aerosmith had sat down with Fairbairn and Collins prior to entering the studio and worked out a formula to return them to the top of the charts. The loveable raggedness was long gone, for now Aerosmith were an ultra-professional act. That was something of a culture shock, even for the group, Tyler admitting, 'Maybe we clarified things, gave some songs a lot of thought where previously we might have left it and said, "Fuck it, that's us, it's cool." That was weird I tell ya!'

If some mourned the loss of the old-style Aerosmith, Tyler wasn't one of them. 'One of the things I didn't like about the old Steven is that when I used to go away and meet somebody new, we'd get so fucked up that by the morning I'd completely forgotten their name. I'd come to and it'd be, "Shit! Where did my stash go? Where are my rings? What happened to my shirt? Who are you?" Being clean, we do more in a day now than we did in a month or even a year when we were getting high. It shows we're doing something right now, having more fun than we had before.' The remaining songs showed just how much fun they were having. 'Angel', the hit that Tyler and Child were determined to write, reached number three in the US and was a mega-ballad, obvious but affecting nonetheless. Only a band in form and fully at ease could wallow in such obvious late 1980s cliché and enjoy it so much.

'Dude (Looks Like A Lady)' illustrated just how much the band had been revitalised by the whole rap movement and their involvement with Run DMC. Jokey, sexy, archetypal Aerosmith, the vocal was rhythmic, the riff simple, the horns kicking along a great slab of funk. This, along with 'Rag Doll', provided the first real glimpse of a new character for Tyler. The 1987 version was using his reputation and the fact that he was still an instantly recognisable face to the limit. It was simply impossible to listen to 'Dude (Looks Like A Lady)' and not picture Tyler's dumb-struck face when the 'she' turned out to be a 'he'. 'When I was fourteen, seven or eight of us piled into a car to go get laid and after a quick roger, wilco and out, on the way back there was this gorgeous thing walking across the street. She got in the car and after five minutes we discovered she was a he. It was that idea and then all the MTV pretty boys that caused me to write the song.'

'Rag Doll' saw Tyler right back at the top, employing the swaggering, slavering lechery, the defiant, flagrantly anti-politically-correct vibe. Classic Aerosmith with an insistent dance groove, it was almost an updated 'Walk This Way', a perfect example of the brilliant pop/rock they'd once been so good at, Tyler accepting, 'It's a departure in a way, but it's part of us that's been lying dormant for years, that bluesiness, a lot of grooves, a pull from the roots.' 'Rag Doll' was extremely witty, probably the first genuinely humorous song they'd done in ten years, the Mae West impression, the jazz scatting and clarinet closing the song in great style. On video, too, 'Rag Doll' worked superbly, as did 'Dude (Looks Like A Lady)'. The videos took all the sexism in rock accusations to their absolute conclusion, overloading it so heavily that it was simply impossible not to find it funny. The politically correct could never admit to it but Tyler was a scream, leaving onlookers with two options – you could either sit there pompous and po-faced saying how disgusting it all was, or you could go along for the ride, taking it all as the harmless joke it was intended as.

Video wasn't a popular medium in the Aerosmith ranks, Tyler pointing out its dangers: 'On "Hangman Jury", we wanted a very specific feel, setting a scene with the porch in the delta, so we put frogs and crickets on there to catch a feeling. But that's a rare thing, songs are usually more general, you can listen to 'em and make 'em personal. Videos take away the beauty of that, it's better to say, "What do *you* think the song looks like?" A song like "Dream On", people have their own feelings about it because it wasn't coloured by a video. If on a record you can do something that makes your mind go, you've really got something going.'

With *Permanent Vacation*, they really did have something going on. The band and producer were genuinely excited by the whole process, Perry energised by the new faces that became involved: 'Bruce Fairbairn was a breath of fresh air from Vancouver. We got excited about working with Jim Vallance and Desmond Child to help with the songwriting. It was interesting that shotgun method, something we hadn't done before. We tried various styles, some

Motown funk, some Yardbirds stuff, it was nice to do some different ideas with some new people. It keeps you thinking.' Tyler agreed, confirming the amount of thought that had been put into the sessions: 'We really tried to make it sound different to the other records that were around. It was interesting when I was a kid to hear things going on in the background, a glass breaking or something, a nice image, neat shit. So we left things in and went on from that.'

On completion, the group concluded that they were totally satisfied with *Permanent Vacation*, reflecting on the distance they'd come over the last couple of years. Tom Hamilton was keen to point out, 'We've become closer personally because of the experiences we've had together and that helps the musical connection. In a way, this record is the next logical album after *Rocks*. *Done With Mirrors* was Aerosmith squirming and fighting to find itself again.' Perry agreed: 'The drugs and drinks put up walls and they've broken down now. We can get on with the music, that's the chemistry. *Done With Mirrors* was a hard record to make, it was a long while since we'd written together and you can't get that back so easy, there were too many preconceptions of what we thought we should sound like and what we thought people wanted from us. There's nothing I'd change with that album because it led to *Permanent Vacation*, that's the way it had to be. Now we're not trying to prove anything to anyone.'

Of course, any new release has to prove itself before the battery of critics. Broadly speaking, it succeeded. Writing in *Q*, Adam Sweeting, not an obvious Aerosmith sympathiser by any means, wrote that it was, 'a good deal cleverer than records like this are supposed to be and I can only urge you to walk this way'. *Hot Press*'s George Byrne felt, 'Aerosmith have basically just remade *Toys In The Attic* with 1980s production values. And, gulp, it's not that bad at all . . . I'd imagine that Aerosmith would make perfect sense in the company of 40,000 screaming Americans and this is ideal listening for people who like to spell rock R-A-W-K.'

Oddly since *Permanent Vacation* was a record that was so defiantly cast in the modern American mode, it was the Stateside critics who were the least impressed. Dennis Hunt, writing in the *Los Angeles Times*, noted, '*Permanent Vacation* is full of perky, somewhat quirky up-temp pop-rock with all sorts of commercial trimmings tacked on . . . once one of the all-time great muscular boogie bands, Aerosmith has gone soft, too fine-tuned, too generously coated with studio-sheen . . . one of the group's problems is that Tyler long ago became an ordinary singer . . . you sense he doesn't mean it. The thrill seems to have gone. Perry isn't the scintillating guitarist he once was either . . . not bad, just disappointing.'

Dennis Hunt's fellow countrymen begged to differ. *Permanent Vacation* was, by a very, very long way the most successful record that Aerosmith had ever produced. Although it only reached number eleven, the album went triple-platinum in double-quick time, spawning three top-twenty American singles. They were back. Indeed, it was as if they'd never been away. Tim Collins lined up 150 gigs for them, mainly across America. If he had had any trepidation over the heavy workload pushing them back into their old habits, he needn't have worried. Joe Perry explained delightedly, 'Now that our private lives are sorted out, you'll find all five of us sitting down at a bar together after a show which you wouldn't have seen since 1974. We were out on the road after we did the new album and we ended up jamming in a club together, which we haven't done for thirteen years. That's how it is now. We try to keep each other straight.' Collins did his bit too, making sure that the mini-bars were swept clean in every hotel room they used, keeping the support bands as far from them as he could. Irony of ironies, Aerosmith found themselves supported in the stadiums by an up-and-coming band of tearaways, Guns N' Roses, a group making the same kind of wild reputation for themselves that Aerosmith had constructed a decade before.

Permanent Vacation had shown that Aerosmith were back on form in the studio. In the course of concert after concert all over the country, they proved that they were back to their explosive best on the stage. Robert Hilburn described their live show as, 'A commanding display of visceral energy . . . the music is built around a traditional hard rock sound – as close in many ways to the pop-minded strains in the Beatles' most aggressive rockers than in the country backwoods blues of the Stones' most influential work. And the band doesn't make any pretence about leading a generation

103

through a dark look at life's forbidden underbelly the way the Stones once did. The only message? Have a good time.'

So it was finally official. The world's foremost good time band had survived it all. Now what? Going up Mr Tyler . . .

11

PUMP-ACTION 45s

The last time that Aerosmith looked to have cracked the rock market wide open, the band had imploded beneath the weight of expectations and the collective stupidity of its members. *Permanent Vacation* had sold so many copies that there would never be any doubts about the personal financial security of the band unless they fell into the drink and drugs void once more. Tyler was intelligent enough to realise the dangers but fit enough to joke about it too, 'I really like the sound of this Ecstasy. Makes me feel like I ought to get my ass along to a meeting real quick!' It's the great truism of addiction that a patient is never cured, but can only go from day to day. The very fact that Tyler had a sense of humour about his problems rather than becoming dourly consumed by them was a good sign.

A further indication of the band's newly discovered maturity came when they finished their mammoth tour in the summer of 1988. Instead of heading straight back to the studio as had been their wont in the 1970s, they took a break to relax, reflect and enjoy their success. They were no longer chasing an audience, so there was no need to work themselves into the state of frenzy that had been at the root of all their problems in the past. Since they'd been busily writing on the road over the course of the previous twelve months, they didn't have the worry of having to start a new record from scratch on day one in the rehearsal room. A short holiday of a couple of months gave them the necessary scope to recharge the batteries, look at the material they had, assess that and produce a few more ideas.

Following *Permanent Vacation* wasn't easy, but it was a more enjoyable kind of pressure when compared with the desperate need to come up with hits that had attended that record's birth. This time around, failure would be a disappointment but it wouldn't be the end of the world. In truth, success was just the tonic that Aerosmith, and Tyler in particular, needed. Never short of self-confidence, to see that arrogance justified in the sales returns in such triumphant fashion was all he could have hoped for. In the past, such acclaim had driven him off the rails, causing him to play the part of the obnoxious rock star to the hilt. Now that he had been straightened out, he could channel all his energies into writing and recording knowing that there was a very appreciative crowd hanging on his every word, dying to hear the next song, the next album.

Things had gone so well with Bruce Fairbairn producing that there was never any doubt that he'd be employed once more. Aerosmith flew back to Little Mountain Studios in Vancouver in April 1989, almost two full years since they'd completed *Permanent Vacation* there. There was no shortage of material, but Jim Vallance and Desmond Child were called in to help fine-tune one or two of the tracks, a sensible move given that they had had such a big part to play in the previous album. In spite of that, their participation was strictly limited. Aerosmith had long memories and if *Permanent Vacation* had been in any sense blemished, it was in providing the critics with sufficient ammunition to accuse them of going soft. The production had been glossy and very crisp, and the roughhouse raucousness that had characterised earlier records was noticeable by its absence. Without wishing to go back on themselves and make records that sounded like they were ten years out of date – they'd done that with *Mirrors*, after all – they were missing out on the rockier side of the band. It made sense that if they wanted to recapture that feel, they had a better chance by writing more of the material in-house. Vallance and Child were craftsmen, songwriters that could hone and polish to perfection. Tyler and Perry were the men you called on if you wanted something with more spit, less polish.

Pump was a much harder vehicle for Aerosmith, with Perry on his best form for a long time. 'F.I.N.E.' was a perfect example of that and of the way in which Aerosmith now wrote and performed. Tyler explained, 'I sit at the drums, Joe's got his guitar and we jam. All the stuff that comes out is stuff that doesn't come out when he's jamming with Joey. Because I'm a different kind of drummer. I know how to ride Joe. "F.I.N.E." was written solely because I sat down at the drums and hit this rhythm that came out of his guitar lick. One inspired the other. Back when we were a nothing band we'd get into rehearsals at Boston University in the basement and we would do things like play "Route 66" and keep rehearsing it. I'd say, "Let's grab that piece there," and that meant we could come up with "Somebody". That's what I bring to the table, my rhythms, my little bit of knowledge, my wondering how the other person did that.' This approach gave Aerosmith a very different quality to other rock bands because rather than sitting on top of the music, Tyler's voice often drove it along. With Perry, a rhythm as much as a lead player, that had always meant that Aerosmith could find a great groove and run with it, turning them into the most danceable of hard rock acts.

'F.I.N.E.' was also notable for the further definition of this new character that Tyler was evolving. Essentially 'the singer' was becoming something of a comic creation, indicating that second time around, they were playing Aerosmith for laughs as much as for any serious pretensions towards art. Even so, there were serious minds at work on the lyric with the seemingly throwaway line about Tipper Gore making a serious point about music censorship. *Pump* was made against a political background of dissent, with the PMRC (Parents' Music Resource Centre) – of which Gore was a leading light – demanding that records should be subjected to rigorous scrutiny, with albums stickered according to the language or sexual content within. Frank Zappa – who Aerosmith quoted briefly on the salacious 'Girl Keeps Coming Apart' – was a leading campaigner in the fight against Gore, but Aerosmith were obviously on his side, nailing their colours firmly to the mast. It wasn't merely a fashionable statement, but evidence of a deeply rooted commitment. In May 1992, they made a donation of $10,000 to MITs (Massachusetts Institute of Technology) Visual Arts Center to replace a grant removed by the National Endowment for the Arts, who had objected to a 'Corporal Politics' exhibit which included human genitalia, breasts fashioned from wax, paper towels and baby bottle nipples. Tyler complained, 'If someone had closed the bars and the frat houses that we played in the 1970s we would never have had a chance to get our music to people's ears. That's what's happening to the arts community, so we wanted to support them.'

They weren't simply interested in defending freedom of speech. They embarked on further pieces of social commentary in the course of *Pump*, most notably with the affecting and effective 'Janie's Got A Gun', one of their finest songs and a thoroughly deserving Grammy winner in 1990. At its heart, it was a song about child molestation, the victimised girl shooting the abusive father. The song took some time to complete, as Tyler explained: 'I went down to my basement to work at four or five in the morning. I was there for five hours trying to come up with something, a little like sensory deprivation, you don't let yourself do anything else, you get into a trance and something comes out . . . I don't sit down and write like some writers do. They think about what they're going to write and then they write it. I just get what comes in at me. It's like I'm a musician and if I can keep my mitt on I can catch the balls that come at me. "Janie" was like that, it just came out, that title and I just filled in the space. I built the ladder rung by rung. I sat for months waiting for the oracle door to open. Then I looked at *Time* magazine and saw this article on forty-eight hours, minute by minute, of handgun deaths in the United States. Then I got off on the child abuse angle. I'd heard this woman speaking about how many children are attacked by their mothers and fathers. It was fucking scary, I felt "Man, I gotta sing about this." That was my toe in the door. When the song was finished I thought it was wonderful that I'd written something that was maybe socially relevant. It was the press that made such a big deal out of it. They went, "Wow, now you guys are into social commentary." It wasn't that big a change in direction. Listen to "Uncle Salty". It may not have the chorus line that grabbed you in the same way as "Janie's Got A Gun" but it was still about child abuse. But y'know, no wonder kids are unhappy and mad. Kids see elephants blown away on television and hear the Los Angeles police talking about shooting people with hollow point bullets and figure, "OK, that's fine, we'll shoot, too." That's why Janie's got a gun. For adults there are non-violent choices, you can get help if you want it, for kids maybe it's harder.'

Without reference to the lyric, the music implied that here was a song dealing with very important subject matter. The instrumentation was taut, Tyler's voice expressive, the thwack of the gun jarring, the solo suggesting confusion and uncertainty. Yet there was a wonderful lightness of touch, a surprising delicacy especially in the wash of synthesised strings and the backing vocals. 'Janie's Got A Gun' could so easily have been pompous or stodgy, good intentions overwhelmed by the seriousness of the theme. Instead it was intelligent, intriguing, reported in an almost journalistic fashion, in a deadpan matter of fact style. That emotional detachment made it all the more chillingly effective. A great record, on its release as a single in America it reached number four, performing a valuable service in bringing a taboo subject out into the public arena.

Aerosmith wouldn't be Aerosmith if the serious wasn't balanced out by some ribald humour. That was available in good measure on *Pump*, the most obvious expression coming in its other huge single, 'Love In An Elevator'. The sexy lift operator enquiring whether or not Mr Tyler would like to go down followed by a speaker flattening laugh established the song's territory, Mr Tyler revelling in the ludicrous nature of his position as a sex symbol. Clearly he took none of it seriously and, so over the top was the video that accompanied it, it was clear that no one else should either. Unfortunately, the PMRC had other ideas and they, along with a number of militant feminist groups protested about both the song and the inevitably raunchy promo clip. Writing in *Hot Press*, Tony Clayton-Lea felt, 'There's sexism here but in a non-threatening sense of the word. "Going . . . down?" enquires the female lift operator in "Love In An Elevator" and really, it's more amusing than insulting. Tyler and company could quite easily have called this album *Hump*, but then it would have prevented them from using the inside cover photograph of a long and shiny petrol pump being inserted into a fuel tank opening. You get the picture.' Fair comment, but Tyler the diplomat was rather more straightforward in his assessment: 'Well, I don't want to offend anyone who doesn't deserve to be, but those feminists who complain about our lyrics obviously aren't getting laid enough. They don't have a lover, they get frustrated and they spoil everybody's fun. It might sound cruel, but if you miss the obvious humour of a song like "Love In An Elevator", I can't see it any other way. Everyone has the same fantasies, they all want to fuck and be fucked.'

Not exactly the explanation guaranteed to endear himself to his opponents, it merely indicated how little Tyler understood the feminist movement and how little they understood him. Admittedly, Aerosmith had been guilty of causing offence in the past with rubbish like 'Bitch's Brew', but this leopard had changed a few of its spots. 'Love In An Elevator' and its ilk wasn't about dominant male taking submissive female, but a celebration of sexual excitement and sexual equality. Not only that, it was, according to Tyler, a true story. "Love In An Elevator" is based on something that once happened to me. I was carrying on in the elevator with someone. The door opened up and it was stopped at the hotel lobby. It was very exciting! The door was open all of six seconds but it was like a millennium.'

Musically it was very close to Bon Jovi once more, but then since Bon Jovi had borrowed from Van Halen, who'd borrowed from Aerosmith, who could tell who was what any longer? The rhythm track was superb, a pumping powerhouse groove, all Aerosmith attitood, with the gum in Tyler's mouth almost audible by the end of the song. 'My Girl' and 'The Other Side' were a couple of songs in similar vein; fun, fun, fun. An adrenalin rush to play and to hear, it was impossible not to visualise the band playing live, Tyler whirling around the stage, Perry watching with detached amusement, busily striking his own poses. This was a band enjoying the natural high life at last, determined to make up for lost time and keen not to miss out on all the great things that were happening to them. After a decade in a chemical haze, it was time to smell the flowers.

It would have been sad if a band that had been through so much hadn't used their experiences to create some songs. 'Monkey On My Back' was the most obviously autobiographical lyric, with its anguished talk of feeding the monkey and having it all and blowing the lot. The performance was really savage, a group angry with themselves and asking hard questions: 'What the fuck were we doing? How'd it happen? Why?' On a different tack, 'Voodoo

Medicine Man', a melodramatic, barking mad blow-out held together by Hamilton's bass asked questions on behalf of the planet, evidence of their burgeoning interest in environmental matters.

'Don't Get Mad, Get Even', a group philosophy, was fun and funny. Tyler's scatting vocals and cod-angry attitude were very enjoyable, but it was the bluesy experimentation that marked this as an important song for them. 'What It Takes' was the obligatory big ballad, the tear-jerking closer complete with heart-breaking vocal and huge, mournful, yearning guitar solo. All the trademarks were present and accounted for and much the same could be said of an album that successfully fused the new professionalism of *Permanent Vacation* to the hard rocking instincts of *Rocks* and the inquisitive nature of *Toys In The Attic*. Most impressive was the level of excitement and commitment they engendered in their playing. After nearly twenty years in the business and with a huge fortune behind them, it was astonishing to hear the sheer glee with which they could attack inconsequential party anthems like 'Young Lust'.

With *Pump* served up as one of their finest offerings, the press were equally enthusiastic. Robert Sandall informed *Q*'s readership that it was, 'A triumphant vindication of the ancient saying that Aerosmith are like a cross between The Rolling Stones and Led Zeppelin, [but that gives no sense of] how purposefully Aerosmith alchemise these into something entirely their own; heavy, guitars-a-go-go rock which stays light on its feet and which swings . . . white rock before all the black bits were removed.'

For the benefit of *Rolling Stone*'s circulation, Kim Neely added, 'Aerosmith continues its winning streak . . . transports the listener right back to the gilt-edged grunge of Aerosmith's wonder years, [recalling] *Toys In The Attic* . . . blends the feel of the glory days with present-day sounds and images with aplomb . . . Tyler's sense of rhythm – perhaps his most under-rated talent – has never been more finely honed . . . Pump up the volume.' Unsurprisingly in the wake of this review, Aerosmith picked up the *Rolling Stone* critic award as the best heavy metal band of 1989.

In *Hot Press*, Tony Clayton-Lea made the point that *Pump* was brimming with 'streamlined, high-octane, accessible rock 'n' roll. It boasts all the tricks of the trade that you'd expect from a band who have been around for a fifth of a century.' Nice review, but the fifth of a century gag mightn't have gone down so well at Aerosmith Towers, reminding them that they were each approaching, or had passed, the big 4-0. Was life going to begin then after all?

Prior to the September 1989 release, Aerosmith's recovery was confirmed by The Hard Rock Café, an establishment that only bothers itself with the biggest and the best. Losers need not apply to join their hall of fame. The Boston Café opened its Aerosmithsonian display featuring a wall filled with artefacts donated by the band. A useful publicity stunt, it alerted the US to the imminent arrival of *Pump*. Within two months, the album had sold two million copies in the US alone. There were very few dissenting voices at this stage, but Jonathan Gold at the *Los Angeles Times* was one of them: 'In this era of decidedly finite sexual limitation people seem to need a shot of Aerosmithsonian bawdiness more than ever . . . perfect rock 'n' roll for the age of limits, great but not awesome, solid but not too original. The riffs are tricky but not all that hard to play. The sexy innuendo of the lyrics is clever but not unapproachably so. Tyler's voice is expressive but decidedly untrained and he has no copyright on the use of scarves. To be a Led Zeppelin or a Metallica requires at least a dram of demonic inspiration but anybody can aspire to be an Aerosmith.'

It wasn't a view that was widely shared, but it did raise a few good points. Much of Aerosmith's second wave of popularity was down to their performances in the heavily-rotated promo videos that filled the MTV screen. Tyler's sexy antics were undeniably attractive to a female audience while male fans aspired to having the fun he managed to have. Yet as Gold pointed out, Tyler was no longer the prowling threat he had been in his prime in the early 1970s. The father of three children, one newly-born, Tyler's leering lascivious-ness, his cartoon-like portrayal of an aggressive, yet safe sexuality seemed all the more important in the post-AIDS world. Tyler acted as an outlet for people's most outlandish fantasies; it was great to hear him singing about sex in an elevator, about young lust, the hot tramp in 'Rag Doll', the super stud making housecalls. Aerosmith were an adolescent escape valve, a cheap erotic novel, a dirty joke. Tyler took his followers out on the sexual rampage that was now off-limits and that made him all the more popular.

112

Was he as popular yet as the great Jagger? In sales terms, Aerosmith were shifting at least as many records at the Stones, now on their umpteenth comeback with *Steel Wheels*. Mick was apparently feeling Tyler's hot breath on his neck, because he started to joke that Aerosmith might just be the warm-up act on their forthcoming tour. Tyler took it in good part: 'I think we're doing a couple of dates with the Stones. Mick announced it. Didn't you hear it on MTV? He was being facetious. I wanted to smack him. "Hey Mick, motherfucker – just because your daughter likes Aerosmith better than the Stones, don't take it out on me." Still, it would be the ultimate.' Secure at last, Tyler could finally admit to the Stones' influence on him and Perry over the years. 'Deep down, we did want to be Mick and Keith. I used to always pretend I was him back in school. And it didn't stop once I got into a band. They were my heroes. We used them as a diving board to dive into the pool of rock 'n' roll. I hated the fact that writers didn't give us credit for what we were doing, always comparing us with them, but on the other hand, I knew they had us nailed. Everything I've done I've stolen from someone. If it's a direct rip-off I do it differently and try to hide where it comes from. People steal from other artists all the time. I'm just honest about it.'

Aerosmith could never escape the Stones analogies and it's probable that they never will. In a funny, roundabout fashion, they even had Mick, Keith, Bill and Charlie to thank for perhaps the greatest coup of their lives. *Steel Wheels* had translated into a live concert extravaganza, crossing the US and breaking box-office records everywhere – a mere four shows at the Los Angeles Memorial Coliseum grossed $9,000,000. The Glimmer Twins, or was it the Zimmer Twins, were forty-six-year-olds by now, Charlie Watts forty-eight, Bill Wyman fifty-three. If the Stones could still pull in the fans in their rock 'n' roll dotage, so too could Aerosmith ten years down the line. With *Pump* having found its way into four million American homes, and the back catalogue still flying out of the shops – *Toys In The Attic* had clocked up five million sales, *Rocks* three million – Aerosmith were looking a very tasty commercial proposition, a fact underlined by their selection as best band in the *Rolling Stone* readers poll announced in March 1991.

Five months later in an astonishing announcement that took the music industry by storm, the Sony Corporation, now owners of Aerosmith's original label, Columbia, secured the band's services in a deal rumoured to be worth in excess of $30,000,000. Tyler nonchalantly remarked, 'That's just what the deal is potentially worth, but it's not what you actually get. It's good to know that we've got a job.' And what a job. The four-album deal provided them with a lavish $10,000,000 advance and a blue-chip royalty rate similar to that enjoyed by the likes of Janet Jackson and, courtesy of the well-publicised 1996 mega-deal, REM. That meant Aerosmith might earn at least a further $4,000,000 per album on top of the advance if their popularity endured.

Yet it wasn't the sheer mathematics of the deal that caught everyone by surprise. The shocker was that Aerosmith still had to deliver a couple of studio albums to Geffen before the deal could actually take effect. A deal signed in 1991 mightn't see its first fruits for six, seven, maybe even eight years! Geffen's President Ed Rosenblatt was disappointed to lose the band but had to confess, 'The Sony agreement involved the kind of investment that we felt made it just not a good business decision.'

As with anything in the business world, this wasn't simply a contract designed to help sell a few records. For Sony, it was a demonstration of their power in the marketplace and a message of intent to put the fear of God into the competition. Def Leppard's manager Peter Mensch best summed up their rationale: 'For Sony who don't have any credible rock bands, it's a legitimate gamble because at last it puts them on the map with rock audiences. Of all the hard-rock bands, Aerosmith has done the best job of crossing over to mainstream America.' Sony were in a prime position to monitor Aerosmith's commercial rebirth, for as Columbia's masters they knew just how well the back catalogue was doing – it was one of the best-sellers in the business. The very fact that they had worked with Columbia in the past was seductive to Aerosmith for it seemed to tie up all the loose ends. It was also sweet revenge – relieving the corporation of all that money less than ten years after it had unceremoniously dumped the band was rather poetic. The group that had been written off as rock 'n' roll casualties had come back to pick up more money than the President of the corporation would make in a lifetime!

Tyler explained, 'I was floored when we first signed the contract, just the fact that anyone would dump that money on the band. It made you feel real good that somebody wanted you that bad. Then I hung it up. I wanted to start rocking again, write the next album, get out and play.' Tom Hamilton was similarly delighted but knew full well that it would do their credibility little good, 'It's a blessing because we know we can live a life of music but its the worst PR move we ever made.' The snipers would be out in force from now on.

Early evidence of the new spirit of collaboration that existed between Aerosmith and Columbia came in November 1991 when they were honoured with a lavish three-CD retrospective box-set. *Pandora's Box* was a compulsive trawl through the band's early history, full of alternative takes, unreleased material, works in progress and so on. *Vox*'s Paul Elliott was delighted with it, rewarding it with a mark of nine out of ten. 'An indispensable collection . . . several of the unreleased cuts are formative versions of songs which later made it on to albums. The early and finished takes are positioned back-to-back which make for fascinating listening . . . just about everything you need to know about Aerosmith, the rock box of the year.' Featuring sleevenotes from the band, their views on some of their greatest songs were a delight for the fans, while their odd little journeys down the by-ways of rock 'n' roll made the set great value for the Aerosmith collector. Giving Aerosmith's work a historical perspective, *Q*'s Mat Snow felt that the imposition of 'hindsight stresses how much more Guns 'N' Roses owe to Aerosmith than Aerosmith owe to the Stones . . . the rhythm section's tough yet funky contribution is too easily overlooked. Even as the songwriting slipped, the rhythm boys motor along greasily.'

All this talk ignores the impact of another tour, one which allowed them beyond the confines of the US at last. They racked up 163 dates this time, taking in most of Europe and venturing as far as Australia. Using an urban roof-top setting – as seen in the excellent video for 'The Other Side' – one of the features was a clothesline, festooned with underwear thrown on the stage by female admirers. Again, this was a nice send-up rather than being exploitive, Robert Hilburn commenting in the *Los Angeles Times* on their 'especially engaging presence: without sacrificing energy or bite, the musicians seem free to enjoy themselves rather than have to put up a hard or unnecessarily aggressive front.' Reviewing a show at Belfast's Kings Hall in *Hot Press*, George Bryne struck one sour note, pointing out, 'One of the drawbacks with this "living legend" lark is that if you've never worshipped at a particular temple first time around, you're unlikely to undergo a sudden conversion fifteen years after the fact, with the result that you're left admiring the people on-stage for the simple fact that they're actually alive rather than for anything they're delivering.' Even so, Byrne warmed to their sense of self-depreciation, noting, 'It's obvious even from the back of the hall that they know that what they're doing is a ridiculous occupation for grown men but at least it beats working or lying on a slab in a morgue . . . "Walk This Way", one of the great riffs, was delivered with a gusto that suggested that they'd suddenly remembered it was them and not Run DMC who'd actually written it.' Any band that can deliver a song it wrote fourteen years ago with real intent is a bit special. It's a trick few can manage. Fewer still can keep coming up with the goods year after year. It's just a question of getting a grip.

12

EAT THE WHO?

With the Sony deal newly inked, the band soon found themselves ensconced in darkest Los Angeles with producer Bruce Fairbairn, beavering away on their next album. That left them in a very interesting but potentially awkward predicament. Aerosmith had a deal with Sony to look forward to, but one which they couldn't move on to until they'd delivered two more full-length albums to Geffen. Working on the first – which was to go under the title *Get A Grip* – outsiders began to wonder aloud if Tyler and the boys might just throw a few old ideas around, pick their way through a bunch of out-takes from previous sessions and quickly cobble together a collection of material that would see them halfway to fulfilling their contractual obligations in double-quick time. Certainly the move to A&M Studios in Los Angeles suggested they wanted to be close to the corporate action rather than locked away in the more creative surroundings of Vancouver.

Those allegations were soon blown out of the water. They worked purposefully in Los Angeles through January and February 1992, but it was clear that their heads were elsewhere. It's not a situation that many can have gone through, but having $30,000,000 waved at you must take the edge off your concentration for a little while. Even if they weren't fully clued in, they still managed to record a full album's worth of material and, if they had wanted to run into Sony's arms as quickly as possible, they could easily have issued the album there and then. Coming off the back of *Pump*, there's no doubt that it would have been a huge international hit once again. After all, Geffen would promote the record enthusiastically, keen to squeeze as much as they could from Aerosmith while they were still signed to the label. With that kind of advertising weight behind them, Aerosmith could be secure in the knowledge that they needn't pull out all the stops.

To their credit, they refused to take things easy. They called a halt to the sessions, thoroughly unhappy about the direction things were taking. In the past, this would have been the cue for fights and tantrums on a massive scale. Now, things were different, Tyler explaining, 'It's important that I can say, "Fuck you, Joe Perry," and not keep it in until it blows up inside me. I can confront him, they can confront me, which they do quite often. It makes things healthier in the studio.' Taking a sensible approach, the band decided to take a break, write some new material, rework what they already had, call in some hired hands to help out, and then reconvene later in the year to complete work on the new project. Fairbairn had prior commitments covering several months through the middle of 1992, so they didn't get to Vancouver until September, remaining there until November.

The extra effort proved to be worthwhile musically, and it also hushed their detractors. The Sony deal wasn't going to make them skimp on the quality control while they remained with Geffen. Everything still had to be just right and if that meant that Sony had to wait another year, so be it. Better they left Geffen with their audience intact than with a dwindling market, punters fed up of being fed below par product. Aerosmith had come back from the grave, rebuilding their reputation with infinite care over the course of *Permanent Vacation* and *Pump*. There weren't about to risk those hard-earned gains by issuing some sub-standard material. One poor album could jeopardise the future – that was a lesson they'd already learned the hard way with *Draw The Line*. If you're going to grow, you have to learn from your mistakes.

If proof were needed of the sense of their decision, it came in the *Billboard* charts for the week of 8 May 1993. Aerosmith's *Get A Grip* débuted in the number-one slot, their first-ever number one, twenty years after they'd released their first album. The band were understandably thrilled with such a great achievement, but in truth

Get A Grip wasn't quite the electrifying collection that *Pump* had been. It seemed a little colder, a little of the spontaneity had gone, the music seemed more meticulously planned, harking back to the approach taken with *Permanent Vacation*. It was as though the extra care taken in the songwriting process had robbed the music of its edge, while the additional songwriters that had been employed detracted from the essential Aerosmith ethos. Once again, there was a sense that the band and their closest allies had been busily analysing everything that was good about Aerosmith, everything that had succeeded in the past and had spent 1992 distilling that into a formula.

Those gripes out of the way, *Get A Grip* was still a very fine record and its multi-platinum sales were just reward for what remained some of the best hard rock released in 1993. With the Sony deal on everyone's mind, only the unrepentant Aerosmith would have opened the album with a song like 'Eat The Rich', termed 'designer class war' by *Vox*'s Max Bell. A viciously angry attack on society's wealthy, it was drenched in irony, for now Aerosmith were rich beyond anyone's dreams and were an undeniable part of the establishment they'd once despised. A solidly impressive starter, few singers could have carried off its incredible verbosity but Tyler's facility for rhythm took him through it with ease. The same was broadly true of 'Get A Grip' which had all the panic, the rush, the confusion and the agitation of city life. These one-time city boys were starting to hanker after a little peace, putting some distance between themselves and the temptations of New York or Los Angeles.

'Fever' followed this breakneck pace, another run through the power of lust, Aerosmith going out in search of a natural high rather than a drug-induced one. The opening power quartet was concluded by 'Livin' On The Edge', another Greenpeace-style anthem. This was a departure in tone for the band, Tyler's world-weary vocal lending a different feel to the proceedings, the backing vocals taking a Beatlesque turn as the instrumentation built to a dramatic crescendo. 'Livin' On The Edge' did indicate that their environmental concerns were genuine, concerns that were brought home to Tyler as wife Teresa presented him with his first son and his fourth child. Fatherhood was now an extremely important part of his life,

119

especially as he had missed so much the first time round. Even so, the incorrigible Tyler still loved his music. 'I listen to the first four songs and I'm so high it's like I just did a line of coke and went out and met the Barbie twins. It's everything that my mind could have come up with, and has been through since I've been old enough to come up with anything. It doesn't mean anything, yet it means everything and at the same time, it's fuck all.' So that clears that up.

The remainder of the album was divided up between typical Aerosmith funk, hard rockers and the ballad – it was an indication of just how much the band had changed over the years that the ballads tended to hold up best. 'Cryin'' was a case in point, the kind of huge sound they'd made their own, fusing emotion with the relaxed swing-beat in which they'd always been experts. With its echoes of 'What Becomes Of The Broken Hearted', it proved nothing more emphatically than the fact that Steven Tyler was one of rock's greatest voices. Technically he might have plenty of shortcomings, but emotionally he was in the very highest class. Almost embarrassed by the tenderness required by the slower material, he tried to denigrate this later by saying '"Cryin'" is the only song I ever got away with that's about a blow-job!' More than that though, this was turning the expected Aerosmith tale of sexual conquest on its head. This time Tyler was the broken-hearted loser having been brought to his knees by a woman, poetic justice after his boasts that that was what he'd been doing to them in a different sense for years.

'Crazy' was a slow blues with a similar feel and theme, progressing at a stately pace towards a particularly eloquent guitar solo. 'Amazing' completed the trilogy in a sense, Aerosmith giving it the full kitchen-sink treatment. From the McCartney-like introduction, this was a heartfelt, powerful song, clearly autobiographical, as Tyler pointed out later. 'I wrote it with a friend, Richard Supa, and back in the 1970s we used to go to the other side of the moon together – I guess we probably lived out there for a few years. When you don't hang out there any more, you kind of don't like to associate with that period, kinda like superstition, but after a while, you realise that you can celebrate that time, it was something you did. This song is pretty much the way it was back then. The more I look back, the more I think there's got to have been a plan for this band, either by a higher power or an angel of mercy. For all the shit I did, someone threw me a rope. I look back on the times I ODed, didn't have any money in the bank, was let go off CBS because the band sucked, couldn't even get my shit together to change my clothes. It's pretty damn amazing, hence the song.' Trotting out a little homespun philosophy – life's a journey, not a destination – it was prevented from descending into twee self-satisfaction by a very witty ending that conjured up the old radio announcements from the 1950s. That's probably the greatest strength of the rejuvenated Aerosmith, their attention to the little touches in the studio that can give a record a life of its own. 'Amazing' was a perfect example of that.

Their other trademark was a unique appreciation of rhythm. 'Gotta Love It' allowed Hamilton and Kramer to shine, the guitarists playing second fiddle as they set up a nice groove with a real 1960s feel. These influences washed over 'Line Up', a brassy romp co-written with Lenny Kravitz. 'Can't Stop Messin'' was a hard rocker, again utilising Tyler's peculiarly rhythmic singing style in a manner reminiscent of Bob Dylan's 'Subterranean Homesick Blues', the '976' line sung in such a bizarre rhythm that it's quite compulsive – the difference between Tyler and the more conventional singing style of Joe Perry, employed on 'Walk On Down', was marked.

With the album in the can after a few problems along the way, the response was extremely gratifying – *Los Angeles Times*'s Jonathan Gold remarked, 'In the 1970s their sound created, more or less, the template for contemporary hard rock, and today's American hard rock bands mine Aerosmith the way the Stones used to plunder the Delta blues . . . *Get A Grip* is 1976 all over again, as if it and not *Rocks* had been the follow-up to *Toys In The Attic* . . . the best Aerosmith album since *Draw The Line* . . . or *Appetite For Destruction*.' *Vox*'s Max Bell worried, 'Maybe Aerosmith are too damn clever for their own good but *Get A Grip* will sell to millions and nag away at the subconscious of those who don't buy it.' *Rolling Stone*'s Mark Coleman was a voice in the wilderness, arguing persuasively, 'Playing it safe according to strict late-1980s directives is exactly what Aerosmith – and its songwriting contractors – are up to.' Nevertheless, he could still see hope for the future, adding, 'Playing together as a band for twenty-odd years definitely has its advantages; each instrumental voice distinctly holds its own in an instantly recognisable blend . . . Remember this band thrives on inconsistency. Its ability to turn a stumble into a comeback is legendary. With all the chartwise calculations and stiffening self-consciousness expurgated, the next Aerosmith album could be a killer. Sometimes, if you wanna get a grip and hold it, you gotta loosen up.'

It was probably fair to say that Aerosmith had begun to take the corporate view of things but having been out on the edge of the rock world for so many years, it was hard to begrudge them their period of relaxation. Having seen the quality of their albums fluctuate wildly over the years, it was perfectly understandable that, having finally found a formula that worked very well for them, they chose to stick with it. After all, how many of us would risk the prospect of multi-million sales with unnecessary avant-garde experimentation? And they were damn good at making that recognisably Aerosmith kind of record, keeping their fans perfectly happy in the process. After all, that was what it was all about now.

Aerosmith took that philosophy on to the concert stage with them too, Tyler pointing out, 'I've always been one of those people who says "I'm gonna give 'em what they came for". I know how I would feel in the back row. I saw Donovan at Carnegie Hall, he was being his quiet self and someone said something in the audience, and he said – I'll never forget it – "You're playing havoc with my senses." What a statement! And he never talked to the audience after that. He played faster, didn't use that vocal effect, couldn't wait to get off-stage. I was let down. I try to remember that when we go out on stage now, 'cos I know we let a lot of people down in the past when we were all too stoned to get it together. Maybe we can make up for that now, we play a long show, we give them the songs we think they'd want to hear. I know I can dance better now because back then I was so completely out of it all the time. I've watched footage from 1978 or something where I just stood there because I was gacked up to the nines. But it's a bit of autopilot now, that way you don't lose touch, and I base that on the times where my behaviour has embarrassed me, things I said to an audience, things I did to a girl or guy I dragged on stage. I try to get it right now. We're still a people's band and that's what gets me off the most. We like what MTV does for us but we didn't need them in the 1970s and we don't need them now. Never will.'

It's already been recorded that Aerosmith's comeback coincided neatly with an increase in the numbers going to gigs in general. Live Aid in 1985 had played a big part in that, as had the advent of the CD where a lot of old records were suddenly revitalised and rediscovered. Tyler was grateful for this shift in behaviour and he was just the man to exploit it. 'I think a lot of people got to a certain age and figured it was time to stop going to concerts, but now they're coming back because they've realised that if you had the rock 'n' roll feeling when you were a kid, you can have it now. The music'll take you back, unlock the door and you can take your jacket and tie off and dance on them. Look at me, I'm supposed to be dead but I'm not, I'm on that stage giving everybody the finger!'

The world tour beckoned, including a second appearance at the Monsters of Rock festival in Donington. The response was uniformly excellent, with *Hot Press*'s Stuart Clark raving about a show at Dublin's Point: 'When it comes to flash bastard rock 'n' roll excess, Aerosmith were out their strutting their not inconsiderable stuff when Van Halen and Guns N' Roses were still deriving nourishment from a nipple rather than Pierre Smirnoff's cure-all elixir . . . this mixture of sweat, danger and camp pantomime makes the 'Smith's live experience so wonderfully compelling . . . during "Train Kept A Rollin'" Tyler executed a perfect back flip and does stuff with the microphone stand that if not illegal is downright immoral.' The tour wound down with the really big show of 1994, Woodstock 2. Having been in the crowd the first time round, Steven Tyler was now one of the main attractions. This time Woodstock was, 'Not as much fun, every time I went out of my trailer I had a million flash bulbs in my face! It was all press, money, TV. Then to finish it off, as soon as I walked on the stage, as soon as I started the first lyric, it started pouring profusely!' But 350,000 fans loved the experience and Aerosmith went back into hibernation knowing full well that they were still top of the hard rock tree.

Importantly for Aerosmith's future prospects, they'd made it perfectly clear that they could weather the storm of changing trends and come out smiling on the other side. Having finished *Pump* in 1989, *Get A Grip* was their first foray into the post-Nirvana world. There's no doubt that the Seattle sound was the most important movement in rock music since punk had emerged in 1976. Oddly, within the rough and ready grunge of bands like Nirvana and Pearl Jam, there were echoes of the roughhouse style of *Rocks*, a sound that Aerosmith had ostensibly moved on from. But in spite of the surface sheen that they applied to their records, Aerosmith were still fuelled by the same spirit that had fired *Toys In The Attic*, something that was more apparent live than in the studio perhaps. Consequently, their concert tour reaffirmed their hard rock credentials and left them in as strong a position as they could ever have imagined possible.

Unlike bands such as the Stones, The Who and, recently, The Sex Pistols, Aerosmith weren't viewed as a nostalgia act but rather as a current band still putting out viable and vibrant albums. Fans went to their shows to hear the latest music at least as much as things like 'Toys In The Attic' from way back when, a real compliment to their new songs. Keeping up to date with the latest developments, they have even released their own CD-ROM game and have also used the Internet to get closer to their fans. Here too, their social conscience has received an airing for going on-line in December 1994, the proceeds from the connection charges went to the Electronic Frontier Foundation (EFF), a civil liberties group devoted to freedom of speech. Aerosmith went so far as to sell Cyperspace tour T-shirts via the net, the cash raised there also going to EFF.

Looking to put something back into the music, they opened a club in Boston – Mama Kin – a venue which books up-and-coming bands and gives them a professionally recorded tape at the end of their show, something they can hawk around the record labels. Alongside that venture, Geffen released *Big Ones*, yet another greatest hits compilation that was a sure-fire hit all around the world.

The current position? At the time of writing, a new Aerosmith album is ready to hit the racks, though its release date has been delayed by management problems. Tim Collins no longer represents the band, which is a shame given his vital role in putting them back together in 1984. Quite what the implication of that will be is anyone's guess at the moment. Whatever the case, there's little doubt that Aerosmith's twelfth studio recording will be one of the hottest releases of 1997. And there's no sign that this train is ready to quit rollin' just yet.

13

CAN'T STOP MESSIN'

Between 1973 and 1985, if any rock fan had heard that a member of Aerosmith had just bought a one-way ticket to the rock 'n' roll crematorium, they wouldn't have batted an eyelid. They might have been saddened but they sure as hell wouldn't have been surprised. Aerosmith attacked those turbulent years with something approaching a death wish. It would be hard to think of any other rock group that had drunk more or taken more drugs in a similar period and survived it. Indeed, compared with the antics of Steven Tyler and Joe Perry in particular, most of rock's numerous casualties had been having a few quiet nights in with the cocoa prior to their untimely deaths. Yet now in 1996, Aerosmith are the proud owners of one of the most lucrative rock recording contracts ever signed. So confident are Sony that Aerosmith have a long and profitable future ahead of them, they are contracted for four brand new albums. At the current rate of progress, that could take the band through to the year 2008 at which point Mr Tyler will be sixty.

Aerosmith have been a singularly accurate barometer for the times they have lived through. In the 1960s, they were busy getting thrown out of school for various minor misdemeanours as the adult world attempted to crack down on a youth culture it didn't understand. In the 1970s they lived the hedonistic life to the full, testing out every sort of drug and drink combination, simultaneously exploring every page of the Karma Sutra and doing sufficient field work to add a multi-volume appendix to it. In the 1980s, it all fell apart and they

126

needed to take account of their ailing bodies. They cleaned up physically prior to cleaning up financially, then went on to devote some of their energies to the environmental and political causes that were suffering in the wake of Reaganomics. In the 1990s, they seem to be casting around for a theme, as seemingly confused and bewildered by the pace of change as everyone else.

Are Aerosmith going to be standard bearers for the next decade too? It merits thought because in the first of the new century, the post-War baby boomers who have set the cultural agenda for the thirty years will be entering their sixties en masse. When they get there, then we're really going to start hearing about what it's like to be old, about the importance of health care for the elderly, the need for adequate pension provision – will Tyler start singing about the trauma of incontinence as a consequence? Age needn't be a problem when it comes to making records. Sinatra's still crooning and John Lee Hooker's growling well past the time he should have picked up a bus pass. Maybe Aerosmith can perform the same feat, though you have to wonder what relevance a bunch of sixty-year-olds are going to have for a teenage market, especially since stage performances will have to be a little more sedate by then. Age is no barrier to playing the blues, but Tyler's are likely to be of the 'got those arthritic hip blues' rather than the more lecherous variety he currently belts out.

The only person who doesn't have a problem with such vision of the future is, predictably enough, Steven Tyler. 'People used to ask me, "What do you reckon you'll be doing when you're forty?" and I told them, "Rocking out and kicking ass!" Now it's "What do you reckon you'll be doing at sixty?" and the answer's the same. I want to be the lounge act on the Space Shuttle so I can sing "Walk This Way" on the ceiling.' Despite those protestations, it's likely that the rest of this decade will see an all-out assault from the band, attempting to capitalise on their Sony deal with the release of two albums, accompanied by some monstrous world tours. After that, things will inevitably cool down a little. Having cheated death once, there's no reason they should go tempting fate. Perry's view is, 'What matters to us is that we have to play great gigs continuously. That philosophy is what we live by.' For the time being, that's a great thing, but as years go by, Tom Hamilton's viewpoint is likely to become more central to the band and their *modus operandi*: 'I don't think we have to compete with trends. Whatever it is this week – grunge, speed metal, whatever – we still get people buying the records. What's important is that we don't think of us as competing with other bands. What really matters is that we can constantly prove that we can write really good songs that people want to hear. That's what being in a band is about. If you can do that, what you do will always be valid.'

Family life will have an increasing pull on them all, as each tries to make some kind of sense of the first half and more of their lives. Drugs and stupidity will loom large in those reflections and the implications for their children are obvious enough. For Perry, that seems to be an almost unbearable burden. 'Somehow we didn't get destroyed but all these people who tried to fly with us weren't so lucky. Believe me, there are plenty of people out there to this day who haven't recovered just because they tried to hang on to us. I think about that a lot. I hate to think how many kids might have overdosed because they saw us using drugs.'

How do you atone for that? Those that have gone are beyond redemption. All that Aerosmith can do is set a better example. They can be used as living proof that the human spirit can fight back from the most terrible disasters – their return from alcoholism and drug addiction shows that, for although having money makes recovery easier, it doesn't make it easy. If Perry and his colleagues could rebuild their lives, then so too can many others afflicted in the same way. Equally, by virtue of their records and their live shows, they can make it transparently obvious that you can have plenty of fun and get a lot out of life without having to resort to dope or booze. Tyler is stating the obvious when he says, 'I'm no born-again puritan,' but he has accepted that he has had to moderate the way he lives for the sake of those who depend on him: 'I'm lucky to have four beautiful kids – they're four, seven, seventeen, nineteen – and I owe it to them to keep myself together. Maybe they'll learn from seeing their dad hit rock bottom and pull himself up again.' With those familial responsibilities to deal with and with more money stashed away in the bank than they'll ever need, why keep pushing Aerosmith to the limits? Tyler once again: 'I need to keep outdoing myself. If an album gets to number one in three countries and sells four million copies, OK, make sure the next one gets to number one everywhere and sells six million. You can always do better and I guess I live most of my life hoping that I'm going to get this incredible burst of inspiration and write the ultimate song. It's an unobtainable dream but that doesn't stop you trying.'

A morality play of almost Biblical proportions, Aerosmith's revival has been described as the greatest comeback since Lazarus. In the end, the essence of this band is simple – the strength of five individuals fighting for the freedom to make their music in the face of some enormous temptations and their own very human frailties. Though they've all indulged in some fierce fights in the studio and on the road, and though the rivalry between the vast egos of Tyler and Perry is the stuff of legend, it's their friendship and solidarity that has finally pulled them through. Sucked in by the industry trappings back in the 1970s, they've seen it all, done it all and don't intend to do it again. They now value their self-sufficiency and certainly aren't going to be taken in by the sycophants that surround them. With a rueful grin, Tyler describes, 'All these people, they come up and say what swell fellows we are and how they knew all along we'd make it. You look at 'em and think, "Jesus, what's going on here? Where were you when we were a cult band?"' Joe Perry is equally cynical when it comes to the bizarre world they inhabit: 'We're not a bunch of kids running around like drunken idiots any longer, but you still have to do certain things because of the business we're in. We're still the same maniacs we always were but we've just added class to our decadence!'

So Steven, has it all been worth it? 'There's nothing in the world, not even hot sex, that compares with the feeling you get when you're up there on stage, the girls at the front are doing their thing and the rest of the crowd are going fucking crazy. This is what keeps me alive. It won't ever change. I'm always going to love Jimi Hendrix – 'Purple Haze' will still give me a hard-on when I'm hooked up to a life-support machine. Hey, even when I'm dead they're going to have a hell of a job nailing the coffin lid down.'

DISCOGRAPHY

ALBUMS

AEROSMITH
Make It/Somebody/Dream On/One Way Street/Mama Kin/Write
Me A Letter/Movin' Out/Walkin' The Dog.
Produced by Adrian Barber.
Released 1973.

GET YOUR WINGS
Same Old Song And Dance/Lord Of The Thighs/Spaced/Woman Of
The World/S.O.S. (Too Bad)/Train Kept A Rollin'/Seasons Of
Wither/Pandora's Box.
Produced by Jack Douglas and Ray Colcord.
Released 1974.

TOYS IN THE ATTIC
Toys In The Attic/Uncle Salty/Adam's Apple/Walk This Way/Big
Ten Inch Record/Sweet Emotion/No More No More/Round And
Round/You See Me Crying.
Produced by Jack Douglas.
Released 1975.

ROCKS
Back In The Saddle/Last Child/Rats In The Cellar/Combination/

Sick As A Dog/Nobody's Fault/Get The Lead Out/Lick And A
Promise/Home Tonight.
Produced by Jack Douglas and Aerosmith.
Released 1976.

DRAW THE LINE
Draw The Line/I Wanna Know Why/Critical Mass/Get It Up/Bright
Light Fright/Kings And Queens/The Hand That Feeds/Sight For
Sore Eyes/Milk Cow Blues.
Produced by Jack Douglas and Aerosmith.
Released 1978.

LIVE BOOTLEG
Back In The Saddle/Sweet Emotion/Lord Of The Thighs/Toys In
The Attic/Last Child/Come Together/Walk This Way/Sick As A
Dog/Dream On/Chip Away The Stone/Sight For Sore Eyes/Mama
Kin/SOS (Too Bad)/I Ain't Got You/Mother Popcorn/Draw The
Line/Train Kept A Rollin'.
Released 1979.

NIGHT IN THE RUTS
No Surprize/Chiquita/Remember (Walking In The Sand)/Cheese
Cake/Three Mile Smile/Reefer Head Woman/Bone To Bone (Coney
Island White Fish Boy)/Think About It/Mia.
Produced by Gary Lyons and Aerosmith.
Released 1979.

GREATEST HITS
Dream On/Same Old Song And Dance/Sweet Emotion/Walk This
Way/Last Child/Back In The Saddle/Draw The Line/Kings And
Queens/Come Together/Remember (Walking In The Sand).
Released 1981.

ROCK IN A HARD PLACE
Jailbait/Lightning Strikes/Bitch's Brew/Bolivian Ragamuffin/Cry Me
A River/Prelude to Joanie/Joanie's Butterfly/Rock In A Hard Place
(Cheshire Cat)/Jig Is Up/Push Comes To Shove.

Produced by Jack Douglas, Steven Tyler and Tony Bongiovi.
Released 1981.

DONE WITH MIRRORS
Let The Music Do The Talking/My Fist Your Face/Shame On
You/The Reason A Dog/Shela/Gypsy Boots/She's On Fire/The
Hop/Darkness.
Produced by Ted Templeman.
Released 1985.

CLASSICS LIVE
Train Kept A Rollin'/Kings And Queens/Sweet Emotion/Dream
On/Mama Kin/Three Mile Smile/Reefer Head Woman/Lord Of The
Thighs/Major Barbra.
Released 1986.

CLASSICS LIVE II
Back In The Saddle/Walk This Way/Movin' Out/Draw The
Line/Same Old Song And Dance/Last Child/Let The Music Do The
Talking/Toys In The Attic.
Released 1987.

PERMANENT VACATION
Heart's Done Time/Magic Touch/Rag Doll/Simoriah/Dude (Looks
Like a Lady)/St. John/Hangman Jury/Girl Keeps Coming
Apart/Angel/Permanent Vacation/I'm Down/The Movie.
Produced by Bruce Fairbairn.
Released 1987.

PUMP
Young Lust/F.I.N.E./Going Down/Love In An Elevator/Monkey On
My Back/Water Song/Janie's Got A Gun/Dulcimer Stomp/The
Other Side/My Girl/Don't Get Mad, Get Even/Hoodoo/Voodoo
Medicine Man/What It Takes.
Produced by Bruce Fairbairn.
Released 1989.

GET A GRIP
Intro/Eat The Rich/Get A Grip/Fever/Livin' On The
Edge/Flesh/Walk On Down/Shut Up And Dance/Cryin'/Gotta Love
It/Crazy/Line Up/Can't Stop Messin'/Amazing/Boogie Man.
Produced by Bruce Fairbairn.
Released 1993.

BIG ONES
Walk On Water/Love In An Elevator/Rag Doll/What It Takes/Dude
(Looks Like A Lady)/Janie's Got A Gun/Cryin'/Amazing/Blind
Man/Deuces Are Wild/The Other Side/Crazy/Eat The
Rich/Angel/Livin' On The Edge/Dude (Looks Like A Lady) Live.
Released 1994.

PANDORA'S TOYS
Sweet Emotion/Draw The Line/Walk This Way/Train Kept A
Rollin'/Mama Kin/Nobody's Fault/Seasons Of Wither/Big Ten Inch
Record/All Your Love/Helter Skelter/Chip Away The Stone.
Released 1994.

SOURCES

BOOKS

Off The Record by Joe Smith, Sidgwick & Jackson, 1989.

MAGAZINES

HOT PRESS
Permanent Vacation LP review by George Byrne, 20 October 1987.
Pump LP review by Tony Clayton-Lea, 5 October 1989.
Belfast King's Hall live review by George Byrne, 14 December 1989.
Dublin Point live review by Johnny Lyons, 6 September 1990.
'Cleaning Up!' by Johnny Lyons, 1 November 1990.
''Smith & Messin'' by Stuart Clark, 3 November 1993.
Dublin Point live review by Stuart Clark, 17 November 1993.

PREMIERE
'Liv For The Day' by Joe Rhodes, August 1996.

Q
Permanent Vacation LP review by Adam Sweeting, September 1987.
Pump LP review by Robert Sandall, October 1989.
'A Quiet Word In Your Ear' by Robert Sandall, November 1989.

Sources

Toys In The Attic LP review by Mat Snow, June 1991.
Pandora's Box LP review by Mat Snow, March 1992.
Reissue Programme review by David Cavanagh, February 1994.
The Q100 Interview by Mat Snow, January 1995.

ROLLING STONE
Get Your Wings LP review by Charley Walters, 6 June 1974.
Toys In The Attic LP review by Gordon Fletcher, 31 July 1975.
'Boston's Aerosmith: Backstage Fighting Men' by Len Epand,
25 September 1975.
Rocks LP review by John Milward, 29 July 1976.
'Leber-Krebs Manage To Make It Happen' by Michael Aron,
25 August 1977.
Draw The Line LP review by Billy Altman, 9 March 1978.
'The Real Aerosmith Bootleg' by Jim Farber, 2 November 1978.
Live Bootleg LP review by Tom Carson, 25 January 1979.
'Aerosmith's Train Keeps A Rollin'' by Daisann McLane,
22 February 1979.
'Random Notes,' 29 November 1979.
Night In The Ruts LP review by David Fricke, 7 February 1980.
'Random Notes', 6 March 1980.
Let The Music Do The Talking LP review by David Fricke,
29 May 1980.
Rock In A Hard Place LP review by J.D. Considine,
28 October 1982.
'Random Notes' by Sheila Rogers, 24 August 1989.
Pump LP review by Kim Neely, 19 October 1989.
'The Band That Wouldn't Die' by David Fricke, 5 April 1990.
'Steven Tyler's Dirty Dozen Stones Songs', 23 August 1990.
'Joe Perry's Top Ten Guitarists', 20 September 1990.
Get A Grip LP review by Mark Coleman, 13 May 1993.
'Talk This Way,' by David Fricke, 3 November 1994.

TIME
'Rock To The Rescue' by Michael Quinn, 1 June 1992.
'Rock Goes Interactive' by Richard Corliss, 17 January 1994.

VOX
Pandora's Box LP review by Paul Elliott, February 1992.
'The High Of The Tyler' by Ann Scanlon, April 1993.
Get A Grip LP review by Max Bell, May 1993.
Reissue Programme review by Stephen Dalton, January 1994.

NEWSPAPERS

ATLANTA JOURNAL
'Tyler Is Enjoying A Healthful "Permanent Vacation"' by Russ DeVault, 8 April 1988.
'Aerosmith's Steven Tyler Shoots Straight' by Russ DeVault, 5 May 1990.
'Aerosmith Plays Hard Rock Of Ages' by Russ DeVault, 1 October 1993.
'Aerosmith's On-line Tour' by Kris Jensen, 4 December 1994.

LOS ANGELES TIMES
'Joe Perry On His Own' by Terry Atkinson, 18 May 1980.
'Joe Perry At The Controls' by Jeff Silberman, 2 August 1981.
'Turn Straight Arrow? Tyler Shoots That Down' by Dennis Hunt, 2 August 1983.
'Aerosmith Stands The Test Of Time' by Matt Damsker, 24 August 1984.
'Aerosmith 86: Reunion Renews That Old Zest' by Jon Matsumoto, 31 January 1986.
Permanent Vacation LP review by Dennis Hunt, 30 August 1987.
'Steven Tyler – Straight But Still Swaggering' by Dennis Hunt, 24 January 1988.
'Aerosmith Draws Line Against Nostalgia' by Robert Hilburn, 29 January 1988.
'Aerosmith: The Rock Of Ages' by Jonathan Gold, 29 October 1989.
'Aerosmith Is Now Rolling On Its Own' by Robert Hilburn, 2 March 1990.
'Aerosmith To Sign Monster Sony Pact' by Patrick Goldstein, 14 August 1991.

Get A Grip LP review by Jonathan Gold, 18 April 1993.
'He Ain't Singin' The Blues' by Robert Hilburn, 18 April 1993.

SOUNDS
Toys In The Attic LP review by John Ingham, 2 August 1975.
Chicago Amphitheatre live review by John Milward, 4 October 1975.
Rocks LP review by Geoff Barton, 5 June 1976.
'Upfront On Aerosmith' by Geoff Burton, 24 July 1976.
Anaheim Stadium live review by Justin Pierce, 25 September 1976.
'This Is Not An Interview . . .' by Toby Goldstein & Geoff Barton, 16 October 1976.
Hammersmith Odeon live review by Barbara Charone, 23 October 1976.
'It's More Fun Trying To Break Britain . . .' by Geoff Barton, 10 September 1977.
Draw The Line LP review by Geoff Barton, 24 December 1977.
Live Bootleg LP review by Geoff Barton, 27 January 1979.
Night In The Ruts LP review by Geoff Barton, 22 December 1979.
'I've Been Through Millions Of Dollars . . .' by Sylvie Simmons, 5 July 1980.
I've Got the Rock 'n' Rolls Again LP review by Xavier Russell, 15 August 1981.